CONTENTS

INTRODUCTION

It does not matter whether your barbecue is a simple, open hibachi, a 'kettle'-style or other type of barbecue with a cover, or a luxurious waggon or built-in barbecue powered by gas or electricity; you can cook beautiful meals on them all, to surprise and delight your family and guests. You may use knobs of ordinary charcoal, prepared briquettes or, for a gas-fired barbecue, lava rock; the results will be equally good, although the way the fire behaves will differ slightly. The shape and depth of your barbecue may affect it too; every barbecue, like every oven, behaves slightly differently, but you will soon learn where your barbecue should be placed and how it should be handled to give you even grilling heat and cooler temperatures where or when you want them.

Barbecued meals are a splendid way for a family to relax or for making guests feel wholly at home. The food can be simple or quite elaborate, served picnic-style or at a table on a serving dish. Either way, it cannot fail to be enjoyable.

BARBECUE EQUIPMENT

Whatever barbecue you have, or whatever the scale of your barbecue — a small family meal or a lavish party — the equipment you
will need is basically the same. You can use sturdy kitchen tools to
start, then buy equipment as you need it.

EQUIPMENT FOR HANDLING THE FIRE AND BARBECUE

Tongs, poker
You will need tongs for spreading the coals and for moving single
lumps of charcoal. Use a poker for flicking grey ash off the fire, but
not for spreading it.

Bellows
Draughts or just the passing of time may cool your fire before
cooking is finished. Blowing on it is hot and dirty work.

Shovel
You will need a small shovel both for putting more coals on the fire
and for removing hot ash afterwards.

Aluminium foil
Lining the barbecue with foil will make cleaning up much easier.

Protective gloves, cloths
NEVER attempt to touch any part of a barbecue or hot pans, forks or
skewers with bare hands.

Sprinkler bottle for water
You must be able to douse any small flare-ups which occur. Use a
bottle with a spray or sprinkler top.

Pile of sand or old barbecue cinders
You will need this for dousing the fire after use. This is better than
water, which may damage the barbecue.

Cleaning materials

COOKING EQUIPMENT

Spit and motor (battery or electric)
This is, of course, optional, but most barbecues except the simplest
hibachis have a place where a spit can be inserted. Many come
equipped with a spit but not a motor. Luxury barbecue may have an
electric spit motor but it ties you to barbecuing within reach of a
power supply.

Drip tray
A drip tray is only essential for spit-roasting.

Meal thermometer
Not essential but helpful if spit-roasting.

Toasting tongs, spatula
You'll need several pairs of tongs. Never turn meat over by piercing it with a fork; always use tongs, or a broad slice or spatula.

Kebab and other long skewers
You'll need plenty for all kebab cooking. Meatballs are best cooked on special flattened skewers. For solid meat kebabs, long, ordinary round skewers are cheap and easy to buy.

Double-sided grill
A double-sided hinged grill which holds the food between two layers of mesh is almost essential if you want to barbecue soft or thin items like burgers or fish which may break up.

Long-handled fork, carving knife, board
You'll need a carving knife and fork and a large board.

Aluminium foil
Also have paper towels and rags available for mopping up drips etc.

Sharp knives
Although it's wise to cut steaks and kebab meats to grilling size ahead of time you should have sharp knives available for doing last-minute trimming, cutting up large cooked portions etc.

Basting brush or mop, jug
You'll need one for each special 'baste' you use and one for plain melted butter or oil. A washing-up brush or mop is a better way to apply a 'baste' than a tube baster because it has a handle.

Gloves, aprons
If just one or two people are doing the cooking, they'll need gloves when handling the grill, hot skewers, etc, and aprons to protect their clothes from drips of fat and basting sauce.

Cooks' table, containers or trays, saucepans
Put the raw food for barbecuing on a trestle table or trolley with a plastic cloth on it. Lay the food in easy-clean containers or on trays. Have bastes, melted butter etc in heavy saucepans which will stand level on the grill (don't use ones with plastic handles).

Protective food coverings
Use decorators' plastic sheets to cover tables etc set up ahead of time. Keep raw food protected from pets and pests until cooking time by laying foil over it with shelves from your oven or cake cooling trays on top.

Spices and seasonings
Besides salt and pepper, offer cooks a choice of dried herbs and spices which will suit the food being barbecued.

SERVING EQUIPMENT

Serving table
Put salads, breads and other ready-to-use foods on a separate table from raw foods, especially if you have a crowd.

Salad bowls, fruit bowls, bread basket, cake cover
Use sturdy containers, avoiding glass or plastic. Put bread or rolls in a basket, not on a plate or board. Keep desserts covered with a plastic cake cover.

Insulated pitchers, jugs
Keep hot foods such as soups or sauces hot in insulated pitchers. Pour a little into a jug as needed.

Bar table, ice bucket, can and bottle openers
Keep drinks away from the food to disperse numbers.

Coffee or tea pot, milk, sugar
Keep coffee or tea hot in insulated containers.

Freezer bag, cold packs
Butter, cream or salads will keep fresher and free from flies in a freezer bag with a frozen cold pack in it.

Serving tools for salads, gâteaux etc.
Use sturdy cheap plastic ones in bright colours to prevent their getting lost.

Kitchen paper, tea towels

Condiments, relishes
Use a big kitchen salt cellar and pepper mill which are easy to spot on the table. Put relishes in sturdy jam jars, clearly labelled.

DINERS' EQUIPMENT

Cardboard plates, mugs

Paper napkins

Cutlery
Most barbecue fare is finger-food but sharp knives and forks will be needed for steaks, extra forks for a salad or gâteau etc.

Aluminium foil, kitchen paper roll
Have several rolls of foil around, for wrapping drumstick ends, etc. Kitchen paper can be used for spills.

Waste bags or bin

Mosquito/fly sprays

SAFETY

Barbecuing is perfectly safe provided you guard against a few obvious fire risks. It is a good idea to make a list of simple safety rules and make sure that children, especially, read and understand them before barbecuing.

SET UP THE BARBECUE IN A SAFE PLACE

1. Site a portable barbecue in the open air, on a patio with one side open to the air, or in a room with all the windows open. Burning charcoal gives off carbon monoxide which are dangerous.
2. See that the barbecue is clear of overhanging trees or low dry bushes, and that the area is free of dry leaves, grass or twigs which could catch fire. Clear up periodically any disposable plates, paper napkins or rags laying around near the barbecue.
3. Do not site the barbecue on slippery or cobbled ground, or on any kind of wooden or vinyl-covered flooring. A level paved or concrete floor is best; make sure the barbecue stands level and is stable on its legs.
4. A strong draught or breeze can rekindle charcoal, and may blow smoke and sparks into people's faces. Put up an adequate flame-proof wind-break, if necessary.
5. Never move a lighted barbecue if you can help it; if you must shift it make sure the wind is at your back.

LIGHT THE FIRE CAREFULLY

Never use petrol, kerosene, lighter fluid, naptha or any volatile fuel to get the fire started. They are not only dangerous, they make the food taste unpleasant.

WATCH OUT — IT'S HOT!

1. Wear heavy oven-gloves to touch any part of a barbecue after the fire has been lit, and even after it seems to have died down. In daylight, it is impossible to 'see' red-hot charcoal; it will appear white and powdery even if giving off extreme heat. The grill and fire-pan can be almost red-hot too without looking it.
2. Don't equip the barbecue with metal or plastic-handled tools, pans or spoons which hold the heat or melt. Use long-handled tongs and other tools if possible.
3. Douse any small flare-ups from dripping fat with a sprinkling of water as soon as they occur, and use a drip tray for spit-roasting. A small pile of sand or old barbecue cinders will smother burning fat.
4. Prevention is better than cure but keep a tube of burn salve handy in case of stinging small burns from sparks or from touching the barbecue accidentally.

FUEL AND FIRE

Most people use charcoal for barbecuing because it is fairly cheap and is easy to use and store, but you can use wood if you want to, say for a spontaneous, spur-of-the moment barbecue.

WOOD

Softwoods such as cedar or birch can be used to get a wood fire going because they burn fast, but the resin they contain makes them smoke heavily, give off sparks and flare easily, so they are not suitable for the main fire. Pine or eucalyptus should never be used, as Australians know well, because they make the food taste of cough-mixture.

Hardwoods such as oak, ash and beech which contain little resin burn more slowly and give a hotter fire; a few sprigs of an aromatic herb such as bay or rosemary added to the fire scent the surrounding air and the food even more romantically than the 'bonfire' smell of the hardwoods. However, if you want a scented (wood *or* charcoal) fire it is usually more practical to buy packeted woods and herbs specially chosen and dried for sprinkling on a fire.

Any wood used for a barbecue or camp-fire must be dry, solid not crumbling, and clean: rotten wood smells awful. A local timber-yard may supply shavings, chips and small off-cuts. Otherwise, use twigs, leaves and bark to start the fire, then add larger twigs and well-dried branches. Pile up a good supply of fuel before you even attempt to start your fire. You will need more than you think.

CHARCOAL

There are two kinds of charcoal: lump charcoal made from both softwoods and hardwoods, and charcoal briquettes made from hardwoods such as beech or oak which are sold in uniform blocks or nuggets. Lump charcoal lights easily and burns fast so is good for getting a fire going, but it may include lumps made from softwoods which smoke, flare and give off sparks. It burns about twice as fast as briquettes so you need twice as much of it.

Briquettes consist of compressed charcoal and may contain some coal waste. They are easier than lumps to arrange in a compact 'bed', being all the same size, and they burn slowly and evenly, giving off an intense heat without smoke or flames — which is what you want for barbecuing. They need less attention, too, than lump charcoal.

It is cheaper to buy briquettes in bulk than in small bags, but you must have a dry storage place for them. Even slightly damp charcoal will create clouds of smoke without really getting set well alight.

FIRELIGHTERS

Lighting a charcoal barbecue fire is child's play using modern fire-lighters. There is no need to use dangerous 'starters' such as methylated spirit or lighter fuel or, worse, to soak charcoal in a bucket of petrol. Unless you possess a portable electric fire-starter or gas blow-lamp, and know how to use it, use either self-igniting charcoal briquettes or the commonplace solid block white firelighters, also available as granules. Jellied alcohol is another choice.

Gas-fired barbecues which are simply lighted by turning a knob are of course foolproof (unless you run out of bottled gas).

BUILDING THE FIRE

Charcoal needs bottom ventilation to get started. If your barbecue has one or more dampers, open them. Cover a solid fire-pan with foil which reflects heat upward, then with gravel which provides a little upward draught and mops up grease spills (you can wash and re-use it). A pair of bellows provides a manpower draught.

Place on this 'bed' either a few balls of crushed newspaper and wood chips (for wood fires); or a few bits (not many) of broken-up solid block firelighter or a handful of granules and some charcoal fragments (for charcoal fires). Cover with a small pile of charcoal (beginners usually use too much). Light the fire with a taper.

When you light your fire will depend on its size, the type of barbecue and fuel and the weather. Briquettes take longer to get going than lump charcoal and any charcoal burns more slowly on a cold or damp day. A barbecue fire for grilling should be ready to cook on in 35 to 40 minutes using briquettes and in 25 to 35 minutes using lump charcoal, provided the fuel is dry. A fire for spit-roasting will take longer. Most manufacturers of larger covered, kettle or waggon barbecues tell you in their instruction leaflets how long to allow for the fire to reach cooking heat. A gas-fired barbecue gives you adequate cooking heat in just 5 minutes on average.

As soon as the fire has caught, spread the charcoal out into an even layer with long-handled tongs. Leave a bit of space at the sides of the fire-pan for more fuel. Always add fuel at the sides, never on top of the fire, because that smothers the heat. Keep a supply of lumps or briquettes warm right beside the barbecue, and add a few to the fire if the coal level burns low.

If you will be cooking for some hours or spit-roasting, you will need more fuel than for a quick barbecued family supper. For spit-roasting, spread the fire across the back of the barbecue parallel with the spit and put a drip-tray under the spit itself to catch drops of grease.

Remember that in daylight the charcoal will not appear to be burning at all. You can only tell it is burning if it has what seems to be a film of white ash on top of the charcoal.

To judge whether the fire is hot enough to cook on, see the

cooking instructions on page 13. If you think it is not hot enough and want to cook quickly, open dampers, flick off any white ash with a poker or give the fire a puff or two of air with bellows. To cool it a little, raise the grill an inch or two, or if it is fixed, move the food to the side of the fire where it is cooler.

DOUSING THE FIRE

Put out the fire as soon as cooking is finished because you can then use the coals again. Don't use water for dousing. It may damage a hot metal or brick barbecue, and the wet fuel will take a long time to dry. Shovel the burning fuel into a bucket or a metal wheelbarrow, then smother it with old barbecue cinders. This method lets you clean up the barbecue itself quickly and you can use the ashes from the fire on the garden.

COOKING ON YOUR BARBECUE

There are four main ways of cooking on your barbecue: open grilling; cooking in foil; kebab or skewer cooking; and spit-roasting.

Open grilling is best suited to firm, flat pieces of meat such as steaks, chops or sausages. Large joints can be partly pre-cooked in the oven, then finished off on the barbecue.

Foil-cooking is used for thin or soft pieces of food which may break up or dry out in cooking such as fish fillets or thin strips of liver.

Kebab cookery is used for bite-sized bits of solid meat or vegetables, or for minced meat.

Spit-roasting by contrast is used for large pieces such as a whole chicken or joint.

FOOD TEMPERATURE

Thaw any frozen meat or fish you will barbecue thoroughly, and bring it to room temperature before cooking. The only exception is thin items such as gammon rashers or chicken breasts. If you want them crusty-brown outside but still juicy within, cook them straight from the refrigerator.

COOKING HEAT

The most important difference between cooking on a barbecue and on your stove is that the level of heat is not automatic, nor the same all over the charcoal 'bed'. Handle your fire so that you get the right degree of heat for your type of cooking. When the charcoal is burning well, spread it in an even layer over the fire-pan with tongs, and leave it to 'settle' for a few minutes before cooking. Test the heat by carefully holding your hand at meat level above the fire. If you can hold it there for 4 seconds without discomfort before having to pull it away, the temperature is probably about 140°C/275°F and you can start spit-roasting. If you can only hold it above the fire for 2 seconds, the temperature is probably about 160°C/325°F and suitable for grilling. Remember that on most barbecues you can alter the degree of cooking heat by raising or lowering the grill, or by opening or closing the damper.

However carefully you have trimmed the meat of fat, drips inevitably fall into the fire, making it flare up. Douse flare-ups when they occur with a small sprinkling of water; they will burn the food.

If the fire cools off during the last part of your grilling or roasting time, raise the grill if possible and flick off any white ash with a poker. Then give it a good pump or two with a pair of bellows, or just from a good pair of lungs, to cheer it up.

OPEN GRILLING

Grilling is the most usual kind of barbecue cooking, and steak is the meat which everyone thinks of barbecuing first. However, other foods can be every bit as good, and the same simple cooking rules apply to them all.

Lamb and pork are particularly good when barbecue-grilled, either in large flat pieces or as steak and chops. Spare ribs, ham and thick gammon rashers are tasty treats. Treat veal like poultry. Grill the other butcher's meats like beef.

Poultry, game birds, rabbit, hare and fish can all be grilled successfully. Venison can be good if marinated. Sausages and burgers are quick and easy to barbecue-grill and always popular.

Use prime cuts
Don't expect a cheap cut to give you tender, juicy meat; use prime cuts of top-quality meat for barbecue grilling. The cooking times are so short that tough meat will stay tough, so will elderly poultry and game.

If you can't afford fillet, rump or sirloin steak you can use chuck steak, but marinate it well first and beat it flat with a mallet.

Oily fish such as mackerel, herring, trout or salmon grill better than white fish, which dry out easily.

Marinate
Marinating the meat will help a lot to tenderise cheaper cuts; so-called meat tenderisers don't do the trick. Take the trouble to make a natural marinade if you can, but if not, use a packeted marinade 'mix' and 'help' it with the end of a bottle of wine or extra long soaking.

Size of portions

The best thickness for grilling portions of meat or fish is 2.5–3.5 cm/ 1–1½ in. Have chops and steaks with bone in cut to this thickness, and steaks without bone if people will grill their own helpings. A tougher cut of boneless meat will be more juicy if cooked in a large, flat piece slowly and sliced after grilling. It cooks more quickly too than 'staggered' individual steaks on a small barbecue. A lamb joint can be split and boned, and laid in a flat thin 'sheet' on the grill.

Small chickens and game birds can be split lengthways, larger ones quartered; solid turkey meat can be sliced.

Cook small fish whole (but cleaned!); cut large ones into steaks like meat. If you want to grill fish fillets or fish fingers, cook them in a double-sided hinged grill. (For quick cooking, you can split whole fish like kippers and cook them the same way.)

Preparing the food

Trim excess fat off the edges of chops; it may cause flare-ups. Snip the edges of thin steaks, chops, cutlets, slices and rashers to prevent them curling during cooking. Unless well marinated, brush the food with oil or melted butter, but do not season it; salt leaches out the juices of meat or poultry and makes it tough. Brush lamp, poultry and veal with plenty of fat.

Cooking the food

The centre of the fire and the grill should both be very hot before you start grilling. As a rule, the grill should be 10–12.5 cm/4–5 in above the fire. When both are really hot, oil the bars of the grill, and lay the food on it. Remember that the centre of the fire will always be hotter than the edges, so place larger items in the centre, and smaller ones around it. Do not crowd them; leave plenty of space around them for turning them.

If you want a well-browned outside crust on your food, and have a movable grill, you can start the cooking with the grill only 5 cm/2 in above the fire, and sear the surface of the food on both sides, then raise the grill to finish the cooking.

As a rule, grill steaks or chops on one side until the top surface is beaded with bubbles, then turn them, and continue turning often until the meat is done as you like it. Baste meat or fish well when turning it, either with a marinade or 'baste', or just with melted butter or oil.

Never turn meat, poultry or other food or test them for readiness by piercing them with a fork or skewer. You will dry them out. Turn them with tongs or with a broad spatula.

Baste with a brush or washing-up mop, not from a jug, to avoid flare-ups.

Season pre-sliced steaks, chops etc, as soon as they are cooked, and add any savoury butter or other topping, relish or sauce. Carve a large piece of steak or other joint on a board and distribute slices. Any condiments, vegetables and salads should be close at hand on the serving table so that the meat can be dressed and eaten right away.

Variations
You can do a dozen and one different things to barbecued-grilled foods to vary them. You can stick herbs in them, rub spices into them, beat them, smother them with a savoury sauce, or weigh them down with a pat of chilled savoury butter or pâté. Some of these flavouring variations sound like torture, and some are. By all means have your favourite savoury butter or sauce at hand for people to use if they wish but don't insist on their use or try to make any barbecue food a set-piece. The pleasure of a barbecue anywhere in the world lies in simple eating. Most people enjoy it just as much or more if they have a plain but well-grilled piece of steak or chop without any fancy extras at all.

COOKING IN FOIL

Cooking in foil packets is an excellent way to barbecue small items such as thin cutlets, lamb's kidneys or fish fillets which would otherwise dry out. The food can be packed and seasoned in the kitchen ahead of time, leaving nothing to do outdoors except put the packets on the grill.

Use a generous piece of foil for each package. Oil or grease it lightly all over, then lay the seasoned and herbed food in the centre of the greased foil, and do up the package securely like a parcel. The parcel must not let juices seep out but try to avoid making thick double folds which may make heat penetrate the foil unevenly.

Foil-wrapped packets can either be cooked on the grill rack or be placed directly on the hot coals at the edge of the fire.

One of the special merits of foil parcels is that they hold the heat for a long time; so they can be cooked before open grilling begins and can be used to feed anyone who has to wait his turn at the barbecue, or who arrives late. Generally, too, if they are not used, they can be frozen just as they are, for an ordinary meal later.

KEBAB OR SKEWER COOKING

Kebabs are known world-wide by various names. Whatever they are called, they consist of small pieces of food threaded on metal or bamboo skewers or wires and then grilled. Usually two or more foods are combined to create colour and flavour contrasts.

Choose foods for skewer cooking which will not soften or flake when cooked; for instance choose firm-fleshed fish. Small meatballs made of seasoned mince are a popular and quickly-cooked kebab item as a change from solid meat or fish cubes. They should be bound with egg or crumbs and not too fatty because as the fat melts they may fall apart and drop off the skewer into the fire.

For each skewer assortment, choose foods which will cook in the same length of time. No one wants to eat assorted 'bits' some of which are overcooked while others are still half raw.

The foods should be cubed, then seasoned or marinated. They can then be put on the skewers ahead of time. The skewers or wires should be lightly oiled before the food is put on them, and the food items should also be lightly oiled just before grilling.

Take care to put the skewer through the centre of each cube. If one side is heavier than the other, the food item will swivel round on the skewer so that only the heavier side gets cooked.

If all the skewer items will cook in the same time, you can if you prefer put the various 'bits' in separate bowls on the cooks' table so that each person can fill his own skewer with the items he prefers. Put a jug of oil and a brush beside them.

As a rule, skewers take a bit longer to cook than solid pieces of meat and fish. Remember to keep them well basted to prevent them drying out.

SPIT-ROASTING

Spit-roasting is a bit more work than the other kinds of barbecue cooking but is always rewarding.

Meat joints or whole poultry or game birds should be marinated and tied into a neat shape securely. Thin flat pieces of meat such as breast of lamb can be sprinkled with stuffing all over the flesh side, then rolled up and tied tightly. Bone-in joints are better boned to make balancing on the spit easier. The hollow left by the bone can be stuffed. Small meat items such as lamb's or pig's hearts can also be stuffed and spit-roasted whole.

Skewer barding fat or fat streaky bacon over a joint covering it; then tie the joint with string at 5 cm/2 in intervals to keep the fat in place and to keep the joint in a neat shape. The skewers can then be removed.

Put the meat or bird on the spit before starting the fire, and rotate it to make sure it is evenly balanced. Spit a joint centrally through its longest part. Spit birds parallel to their backbones bringing the end of the spit out between legs and tail. Once balanced, keep the meat aside, still on the spit, until ready to barbecue.

Use a meat thermometer if possible when spit-roasting if you want all the meat fully cooked before serving. If you like, however, you can carve the outside slices of a joint still on the spit before it is fully cooked through, and leave the half-raw meat exposed, to go on cooking.

The fire should be near the back of the barbecue. Place a drip pan in front, under the meat, taking care that there are no hot coals or ashes under the pan. Baste the meat with the pan juices and with butter or oil.

KETTLE COOKING

Any barbecue cooking method can be used with success in a barbecue kettle — a barbecue with a lid; although spit-roasting is not used because even large items such as a turkey can simply be placed on the grill, and the lid closed. It then holds in the heat, so that the food cooks in the same way as in an oven.

If you have a kettle and use this method, you can also 'smoke-cook' the food by adding wood chips to the charcoal, or 'steam-book' it by standing a pan of water on the grill beside it. Steam-cooking helps to keep large items of food moist and succulent.

For closed-kettle cooking, use the same roasting times that you would use in an ordinry oven, as soon as the fire has really got going.

GAS-FIRED COOKING

Gas-fired barbecues usually have two controls, high and low, giving you a choice of easily-managed heats. You will probably find that you can cook most foods on the lower heat, and keep the high heat mostly for 'instant' browning.

NOTES ON THE RECIPES

All the recipes in the book are designed to serve four, unless otherwise specified.

All spoon measurements are level, and are based on a 5 ml teaspoon and a 15 ml tablespoon.

Follow one set of measurements only. Do not mix metric, imperial and American measures.

The following symbols are used at the beginning of recipes.

 Suitable for freezing for the time specified.

 Suitable for an open grill.

 Suitable for a covered grill.

Before you Light the Fire

MARINADES, BASTES AND BUTTERS

A marinade will tenderise and flavour your meat, and make it suitable for grilling. A baste will keep it moist and succulent while cooking, and a savoury butter will replace the fat lost in drippings, and give extra flavour.

Always marinate meat in a non-metallic dish; use a ceramic, plastic or enamelled one, for example. Some cooks marinate meat in a large, securely closed plastic bag placed in a shallow dish; it makes it easier to turn the meat over in the marinade, to soak all parts of it. When you brush a baste on food while grilling, remember that heat melts nylon bristles; some cooks sprinkle the baste on from a ladle.

Marinades and bastes, like salad dressings and dips, are not suitable for freezing if they contain fresh flavourings such as onion, garlic or fresh herbs. Nor are butters. Other marinades, bastes and butters can be frozen for up to one month.

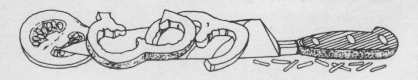

BEEF MARINADES

Allow meat to marinate for at least 1 hour in the mixed ingredients of any of the following marinades; turn it several times so that the flavours penetrate thoroughly. These marinades will tenderise most meat cuts, but tough cuts may benefit by being beaten out first.

Herb-Wine Marinade and Baste

INGREDIENTS	Metric	Imperial	American
Tomato ketchup (catsup)	65 ml	2½ fl oz	⅓ cup
Salad oil	125 ml	4 fl oz	½ cup
Dry red wine	175 ml	6 fl oz	¾ cup
Dried onion flakes, soaked	1 tbsp	1 tbsp	1 tbsp
Worcestershire sauce	1 tbsp	1 tbsp	1 tbsp
Crushed dried rosemary	1 tsp	1 tsp	1 tsp
Salt	1½ tsp	1½ tsp	1½ tsp
Black pepper	¼ tsp	¼ tsp	¼ tsp

Teriyaki Marinade

INGREDIENTS	Metric	Imperial	American
Salad oil	2 tbsp	2 tbsp	2 tbsp
Soy sauce	65 ml	2½ fl oz	⅓ cup
Soft brown sugar	2 tbsp	2 tbsp	2 tbsp
Dry sherry or Japanese saké	1 tbsp	1 tbsp	1 tbsp
Grated fresh ginger root	1 tsp	1 tsp	1 tsp
OR	OR	OR	OR
Ground ginger	¼ tsp	¼ tsp	¼ tsp
Garlic clove, grated or squeezed (minced or pressed)	1	1	1

Wine and Garlic Marinade

INGREDIENTS	Metric	Imperial	American
Dry red wine	225 ml	8 fl oz	1 cup
Red wine vinegar	2 tbsp	2 tbsp	2 tbsp
Garlic cloves, grated or squeezed (minced or pressed)	2	2	2
Dried oregano leaves	1 tsp	1 tsp	1 tsp
Salad oil	2 tbsp	2 tbsp	2 tbsp

FLAVOURED BUTTERS FOR BEEF

Use these flavoured butters to season barbecued meats during grilling or just before serving. Most are not intended for long-term storage; for quality flavour, use within 1–2 weeks. Do not freeze.

Shallot Butter

INGREDIENTS	Metric	Imperial	American
Butter (unsalted)	2 tbsp	2 tbsp	2 tbsp
Medium-sized onion, finely chopped	1	1	1
Dry sherry	2 tbsp	2 tbsp	2 tbsp
Butter or margarine at room temperature	125 g	4 oz	½ cup
Salt	¼ tsp	¼ tsp	¼ tsp

Melt the 2 tbsp unsalted butter in a frying pan, add the chopped onion and fry until soft. Add the sherry and simmer until evaporated. Cool the mixture, then mix in a bowl with the butter or margarine and salt, and beat until light and fluffy. Cover and refrigerate until needed.

Fines Herbes Butter

INGREDIENTS	Metric	Imperial	American
Butter or margarine, softened	125 g	4 oz	½ cup
Chopped parsley	1 tbsp	1 tbsp	1 tbsp
Chopped fresh chives	1 tbsp	1 tbsp	1 tbsp
Dried tarragon (leaves)	½ tsp	½ tsp	½ tsp
Dried chervil	½ tsp	½ tsp	½ tsp
Salt	¼ tsp	¼ tsp	¼ tsp
Pinch of black pepper			

Beat all the ingredients together until light and fluffy. Cover and refrigerate until needed.

Garlic Butter

INGREDIENTS	Metric	Imperial	American
Butter or margarine, softened	125 g	4 oz	½ cup
Garlic cloves, grated or squeezed (Minced or pressed)	2–3	2–3	2–3
Finely chopped parsley	2 tbsp	2 tbsp	2 tbsp

Beat all the ingredients together until light and fluffy. Cover and refrigerate until needed.

Red Onion Butter

INGREDIENTS	Metric	Imperial	American
Butter (unsalted)	2 tbsp	2 tbsp	2 tbsp
Medium-sized mild onion (use a red onion for choice), finely chopped	1	1	1
OR	OR	OR	OR
Shallots	2	2	2
Dry red wine	2 tbsp	2 tbsp	2 tbsp
Butter or margarine, softened	125 g	4 oz	½ cup
Salt	¼ tsp	¼ tsp	¼ tsp

Melt the unsalted butter in a frying pan, and fry the chopped onion or shallots until soft. Add the wine, and simmer until evaporated. Cool thoroughly, then mix with the softened fat and salt. Process in a blender or beat until light and fluffy. Cover and refrigerate until needed.

LAMB MARINADES

Barbecued lamb or other meats can be varied just by varying the marinade or baste you use: and the only real difference between these two forms of seasoning is that the meat is steeped in a marinade before cooking, and is brushed or sprinkled with a baste during and after cooking. A marinade, which is designed to tender-ise the meat, always contains an acid such as vinegar, wine or lemon juice.

Easy Lamb Marinade

INGREDIENTS	Metric	Imperial	American
Dry sherry or apple juice	125 ml	4 fl oz	½ cup
Olive oil or salad oil	50 ml	2 fl oz	¼ cup
Salt	2 tsp	2 tsp	2 tsp
Dried oregano	2 tsp	2 tsp	2 tsp
Black pepper	½ tsp	½ tsp	½ tsp
Large onion, sliced	1	1	1

Combine all the ingredients. Pour over the lamb. Cover, and chill for up to 4 hours, turning meat over occasionally.

Honey and Wine Marinade

INGREDIENTS	Metric	Imperial	American
Butter (unsalted)	2 tbsp	2 tbsp	2 tbsp
Dry white wine	225 ml	8 fl oz	1 cup
White wine vinegar	2 tbsp	2 tbsp	2 tbsp
Clear honey	75 g	3 oz	$\frac{1}{3}$ cup
Fresh or dried chopped mint	1 tsp	1 tsp	1 tsp
Salt	1 tsp	1 tsp	1 tsp
Garlic cloves, grated or squeezed (minced or pressed)	2	2	2

Melt the butter in a saucepan, and add the remaining ingredients. Pour over lamb chops, shanks or breast and marinate for up to 4 hours. Use any marinade not absorbed to baste the meat during cooking.

LAMB BASTES

Mediterranean Leg of Lamb Baste

INGREDIENTS	Metric	Imperial	American
Garlic cloves, cut into slivers	4	4	4
Butter or margarine	4 tbsp	4 tbsp	4 tbsp
Lemon juice	3 tbsp	3 tbsp	3 tbsp
Dried oregano (leaves)	$\frac{1}{2}$ tsp	$\frac{1}{2}$ tsp	$\frac{1}{2}$ tsp

Before cooking, insert the garlic slivers into small slits made in the meat with a small pointed knife. For the baste, melt the fat, and add the lemon juice and herbs. Brush the baste over the meat occasionally while cooking.

Parsley-Orange Baste

INGREDIENTS	Metric	Imperial	American
Butter or margarine	125 g	4 oz	$\frac{1}{2}$ cup
Grated orange rind	2 tbsp	2 tbsp	2 tbsp
Finely chopped parsley	2 tbsp	2 tbsp	2 tbsp
Clear honey	2 tbsp	2 tbsp	2 tbsp
Lemon juice	50 ml	2 fl oz	$\frac{1}{4}$ cup
Salt	$\frac{1}{2}$ tsp	$\frac{1}{2}$ tsp	$\frac{1}{2}$ tsp

Melt the fat in a saucepan, then add the remaining ingredients. Use to brush on the meat while cooking.

PORK MARINADES

Soy-Flavoured Marinade

INGREDIENTS	Metric	Imperial	American
Chicken stock	125 ml	4 fl oz	$\frac{1}{2}$ cup
Soy sauce	125 ml	4 fl oz	$\frac{1}{2}$ cup
Dry sherry or Japanese saké	50 ml	2 fl oz	$\frac{1}{4}$ cup
Sugar	6 tbsp	6 tbsp	6 tbsp
Garlic, grated or squeezed (minced or pressed)	1 tsp	1 tsp	1 tsp

Mix all the ingredients, and pour the mixture over the pork. Cover, and refrigerate for at least 24 hours, turning the meat over occasionally.

Beer Marinade

INGREDIENTS	Metric	Imperial	American
Dark strong beer	275 ml	$\frac{1}{2}$ pt	$1\frac{1}{4}$ cups
Black pepper	$\frac{1}{4}$ tsp	$\frac{1}{4}$ tsp	$\frac{1}{4}$ tsp
Onions, thinly sliced	3	3	3
Bay leaf	1	1	1
Black treacle (black-strap molasses), warmed	50 ml	2 fl oz	$\frac{1}{4}$ cup

Mix all the ingredients, and pour over the meat. Cover and refrigerate overnight.

PORK BASTES

Apricot Baste

INGREDIENTS	Metric	Imperial	American
Apricots or peaches canned in syrup	298 g can	11 oz can	11 oz can
Tomato ketchup (catsup)	50 ml	2 fl oz	$\frac{1}{4}$ cup
Lemon juice	3 tbsp	3 tbsp	3 tbsp
Salad oil or melted butter	2 tbsp	2 tbsp	2 tbsp
Salt	$\frac{1}{2}$ tsp	$\frac{1}{2}$ tsp	$\frac{1}{2}$ tsp
Pinch of grated lemon rind			

Prepare and use like the Savoury Raisin Baste overleaf.

Savoury Raisin Baste

INGREDIENTS	Metric	Imperial	American
Seedless raisins, chopped	75 g	3 oz	$\frac{1}{2}$ cup
Onion, chopped	40 g	1$\frac{1}{2}$ oz	$\frac{1}{4}$ cup
Garlic clove, grated or squeezed (minced or pressed)	1	1	1
Tomato ketchup (catsup)	125 ml	4 fl oz	$\frac{1}{2}$ cup
Beef stock or dry white wine	125 ml	4 fl oz	$\frac{1}{2}$ cup
Salad oil	3 tbsp	3 tbsp	3 tbsp
Wine vinegar	2 tbsp	2 tbsp	2 tbsp
Soft brown sugar	1 tbsp	1 tbsp	1 tbsp
Made mustard	1 tsp	1 tsp	1 tsp
Salt	$\frac{1}{2}$ tsp	$\frac{1}{2}$ tsp	$\frac{1}{2}$ tsp
Pinch of dried dill leaves			

Simmer all the ingredients in a saucepan for 10–15 minutes, and use to baste the meat while cooking.

POULTRY MARINADES

Basic Wine Marinade

INGREDIENTS	Metric	Imperial	American
Onions, coarsely chopped	2	2	2
Garlic cloves, chopped	3	3	3
Black pepper	1 tsp	1 tsp	1 tsp
Pinch of cayenne pepper			
White wine vinegar	125 ml	4 fl oz	$\frac{1}{2}$ cup
Dry white wine	225 ml	8 fl oz	1 cup
Salad oil	50 ml	2 fl oz	$\frac{1}{4}$ cup
Crushed dried thyme leaves	1$\frac{1}{2}$ tsp	1$\frac{1}{2}$ tsp	1$\frac{1}{2}$ tsp
Grated lemon rind	$\frac{1}{2}$ tsp	$\frac{1}{2}$ tsp	$\frac{1}{2}$ tsp
Lemon juice	2 tbsp	2 tbsp	2 tbsp
Clear honey	1 tsp	1 tsp	1 tsp

Mix all the ingredients. Use as they are, or process in a food processor or electric blender to make a thicker marinade. Pour the mixture over poultry pieces, and marinate for about 2 hours, then drain. Use the liquid to baste the poultry while cooking.

Ginger-Soy Marinade

INGREDIENTS	Metric	Imperial	American
Salad oil	2 tbsp	2 tbsp	2 tbsp
Soy sauce	65 ml	2½ fl oz	⅓ cup
Clear honey or soft brown sugar	2 tbsp	2 tbsp	2 tbsp
Red wine vinegar	1 tbsp	1 tbsp	1 tbsp
Fresh ginger root, grated	1 tsp	1 tsp	1 tsp
Garlic clove, grated or squeezed (minced or pressed)	1	1	1

Mix all the ingredients and use to marinate poultry pieces for 4–8 hours. Use as a baste while they cook too. (This marinade can also be used for a whole bird and is good with duck.)

POULTRY BASTES

Herb Butter Baste

INGREDIENTS	Metric	Imperial	American
Melted butter or margarine	6 tbsp	6 tbsp	6 tbsp
Garlic clove, grated or squeezed (minced or pressed)	1	1	1
Black pepper	¾ tsp	¾ tsp	¾ tsp
Dried thyme leaves, sage leaves, oregano, marjoram leaves, basil leaves	½ tsp each	½ tsp each	½ tsp each

Mix all the ingredients, and use to baste poultry while cooking.

Green Onion Baste

INGREDIENTS	Metric	Imperial	American
Butter or margarine, softened	225 g	8 oz	1 cup
Finely chopped parsley	3 tbsp	3 tbsp	3 tbsp
Spring onion (scallion), green and white parts, finely chopped	3 tbsp	3 tbsp	3 tbsp
Dry mustard power	¾ tsp	¾ tsp	¾ tsp
Dried mixed herbs	¾ tsp	¾ tsp	1 tsp
Garlic powder	¼ tsp	¼ tsp	¼ tsp
A few drops of Tabasco or chilli sauce			
Pinch of black pepper			

Mix all the ingredients. Use to baste any poultry.

SEAFOOD MARINADES

The following flavoursome marinades and bastes can be used on fish fillets, steaks or small whole fish. Each recipe makes enough marinade or baste for 900 g–1.4 kg/2–3 lb of fish.

Japanese Teriyaki Marinade

INGREDIENTS	Metric	Imperial	American
Soy sauce	125 ml	4 fl oz	½ cup
Sugar	1 tbsp	1 tbsp	1 tbsp
Lemon juice	2 tsp	2 tsp	2 tsp
Grated fresh ginger root or ground ginger	2 tsp	2 tsp	2 tsp
Worcestershire sauce	1 tsp	1 tsp	1 tsp
Garlic powder	1 tsp	1 tsp	1 tsp
Garlic clove, grated or squeezed (minced or pressed)	1	1	1
Dry sherry or Japanese saké	2 tbsp	2 tbsp	2 tbsp

Mix all the ingredients, and pour over the fish. Cover, and refrigerate for 30 minutes–2 hours, turning fish occasionally.

Herb and Wine Marinade

INGREDIENTS	Metric	Imperial	American
Dry white wine	225 ml	8 fl oz	1 cup
Lemon juice	50 ml	2 fl oz	¼ cup
White wine vinegar	2 tbsp	2 tbsp	2 tbsp
Garlic cloves, grated or squeezed (minced or pressed)	2	2	2
Dried tarragon leaves or crushed rosemary	1 tsp	1 tsp	1 tsp
Melted butter or margarine, or salad oil	2 tbsp	2 tbsp	2 tbsp

Mix the ingredients in a small saucepan. Heat to simmering point, remove from the heat, and leave to stand for 1 hour. Pour the mixture over the fish. Cover, and refrigerate for 30–60 minutes, turning the fish once or twice.

Orange-Soy Marinade

INGREDIENTS	Metric	Imperial	American
Soy sauce	125 ml	4 fl oz	½ cup
Orange juice	125 ml	4 fl oz	½ cup
Tomato ketchup (catsup)	50 ml	2 fl oz	¼ cup
Finely chopped parsley	20 g	¾ oz	¼ cup
Garlic cloves, grated or squeezed (minced or pressed)	2	2	2
Lemon juice	2 tbsp	2 tbsp	2 tbsp
Black pepper	¼ tsp	¼ tsp	¼ tsp

Mix the ingredients and pour over the fish. Cover, and refrigerate for 30–60 minutes.

SEAFOOD BASTES

Seafood Butter Baste

INGREDIENTS	Metric	Imperial	American
Melted butter or margarine	50 g	2 oz	¼ cup
Lemon juice, dry sherry or dry white vermouth	50 ml	2 fl oz	¼ cup
Dried tarragon leaves	½ tsp	½ tsp	½ tsp
OR	OR	OR	OR
Dried rosemary and thyme leaves	¼ tsp each	¼ tsp each	¼ tsp each

Mix the chosen ingredients, and use to baste the fish often during cooking.

Lemon and Onion Baste

INGREDIENTS	Metric	Imperial	American
Lemon juice	125 ml	4 fl oz	½ cup
Salad oil	50 ml	2 fl oz	¼ cup
Salt	¼ tsp	¼ tsp	¼ tsp
Sugar	¼ tsp	¼ tsp	¼ tsp
Pinch of black pepper			
Spring onion (green stem) chopped (scallion, green stem)	2 tbsp	2 tbsp	2 tbsp

Mix the ingredients, and use to baste the fish often during cooking.

BREADS

Hot buttered French bread, with or without garlic, is a reliable standby for outdoor meals. Other breads, such as rye bread or fruit bread, can also be warmed on a barbecue grill if wrapped in foil. If you have a big covered grill, you can even bake bread on the barbecue, and serve it freshly baked. Any baking powder bread ('quick' bread) can be cooked alongside the meat in this way.

To bake bread, you will need a mercury-type oven thermometer placed on the edge of the grill to help you to maintain a constant temperature of 180°C/350°F. The grill should be 10–15 cm/4–6 in above a solid bed of medium-hot coals. Check the temperature about every 15 minutes. Place the bread tin (pan) on the coolest part of the grill, not directly over the hot coals, and turn it round often so that the bread cooks evenly. Use your own favourite recipes for quick breads or try the Parmesan Onion Bread recipe below.

Grilled French Bread

6 weeks (without garlic)

INGREDIENTS	Metric	Imperial	American
Butter or margarine, softened	125 g	4 oz	½ cup
Garlic cloves, grated or squeezed (minced or pressed) optional	3	3	3
Stick of French bread (450 g/ 1 lb) split lengthways	1	1	1

Melt the fat in a small pan over medium heat. Add the garlic if you wish. Brush the melted fat over the cut sides of the bread. Place the halves, cut side down, on the grill, 10–15 cm/4–6 in over medium-hot coals for about 5 minutes. Cut into 5 cm/2 in pieces for serving.

Foil-Wrapped Bread

6 weeks

INGREDIENTS	Metric	Imperial	American
Butter or margarine, melted	125 g	4 oz	½ cup
Loaf of bread (any kind), weighing about 450 g/1 lb split lengthways or sliced	1	1	1

Brush melted fat over the cut sides of a split loaf or on one side of each slice. Reassemble the loaf, and wrap tightly in a doubled sheet of heavy duty foil. Place on the barbecue grill 10–15 cm/4–6 in above medium-hot coals for 10–12 minutes. If required, cut in slices to serve.

Parmesan Onion Bread

INGREDIENTS	Metric	Imperial	American
Plain white flour	225 g	8 oz	2 cups
Baking powder	2 tsp	2 tsp	2 tsp
Salt	½ tsp	½ tsp	½ tsp
Grated Parmesan cheese	75 g	3 oz	¾ cup
Butter or margarine	50 g	2 oz	¼ cup
Melted butter	1 tbsp	1 tbsp	1 tbsp
Spring onion (green stem) finely sliced (scallion, green stem)	125 g	4 oz	⅔ cup
Garlic cloves, grated or squeezed (minced or pressed)	2	2	2
Celery, caraway or toasted sesame seeds	1 tbsp	1 tbsp	1 tbsp
Egg	1	1	1
Milk	175 ml	6 fl oz	¾ cup
Fat for greasing			

Stir together in a bowl the flour, baking powder salt and Parmesan. Cut or rub in the solid fat until the mixture resembles coarse crumbs. Use the melted fat to fry the onion and garlic until soft. Add them to the flour mixture with the seeds. Beat the egg into the milk, and use to bind the mixture, blending fully. Grease a 22 cm/9 in round or square baking tin (pan), turn in the dough and level the top. Bake in a kettle-style covered barbecue at 180°C/350°F for about 1 hour, until bread is risen and crusty, and begins to shrink from the sides of the pan. Turn out onto a wire rack, and cool until easy to cut into thick slices or wedges with a serrated knife.

    Serves 8.
    Do not freeze.

STARTERS & NIBBLERS

Although your barbecue entertaining should be as simple as poss-ible, one or two 'easy-to-eat' starters are essential. Even small barbecued items take time to cook, and people, especially children, get restless when they're hungry and smell the good cooking.

Mugs of warming soup are excellent on a chilly evening. At other times the best starter of all is not a set-piece dish but just a choice of raw and blanched vegetables arranged in a picture book pattern on one or two trays. They're easy to pick up and eat while waiting one's turn to barbecue, and their fresh crispness contrasts well with the charcoal-grilled foods. You'll find that people will come back and pick up 'nibblers' between eating barbecued items too, so prepare plenty.

Offer a choice of dips with the vegetables. People come back to these as well, and use them instead of a sauce with their barbecued foods or as salad dressings.

Have one or two small dishes of other 'nibblers' around. Salted nuts, crisps, olives or cheese straws are always popular or, for a slightly more solid 'nibbler' try Ham and Cheese Fingers.

Scandinavian Pea Soup

 2 months

INGREDIENTS	Metric	Imperial	American
Butter	25 g	1 oz	2 tbsp
Streaky bacon rashers without rind, chopped	50 g	2 oz	$\frac{1}{4}$ cup
Large onion, chopped	1	1	1
Yellow split peas, washed	125 g	4 oz	4 oz
Chicken stock	900 ml	1$\frac{1}{2}$ pt	4 cups (scant)

Salt and ground black pepper

Melt the butter in a heavy stewpan, and fry the chopped bacon and onion until soft. Add the peas and stock and season well. Cover and simmer for 1$\frac{1}{2}$ hours or pressure cook for 11 minutes. Put the peas in batches in an electric blender with a little stock and process until smooth. Mix with the rest of the stock. Reheat when needed and pour into a large vacuum flask. Seal securely. Serve in mugs.

Ham and Cheese Fingers

 2 weeks

INGREDIENTS	Metric	Imperial	American
Flour	225 g	8 oz	2 cups
Margarine	125 g	4 oz	½ cup
Cold water	2 tbsp	2 tbsp	2 tbsp
Ham or gammon, finely shredded	125 g	4 oz	½ cup
Soft white breadcrumbs	50 g	2 oz	1 cup
Tomato purée (paste)	1 tsp	1 tsp	1 tsp
Sprinkling of dry mustard			
Grated cheese	125 g	4 oz	½ cup
Beaten egg			

Sift the flour into a bowl. Rub in the fat until the mixture resembles breadcrumbs. Bind to a pliant pastry with the water. Knead lightly, then roll out on a floured surface into a 30 cm/12 in square. Cut the square into 2 equal rectangles. Chill for 15 minutes. Heat the oven to 220°C/425°F/Gas Mark 7.

Place one rectangle on a damped baking sheet. Blend thoroughly the ham or gammon, breadcrumbs, tomato paste and mustard. Spread on the pastry on the baking sheet, leaving 1 cm/½ in of the edge bare all round. Scatter the cheese on top. Brush the edges of the pastry with egg, and fit on the second piece of pastry to make a lid. Seal the edges. Brush the top of the pastry with egg. Bake for 25–30 minutes. Cool, then cut into 12 fingers.

Cheese Straws

 2 months

INGREDIENTS	Metric	Imperial	American
Butter, softened	125 g	4 oz	½ cup
Flour	125 g	4 oz	1 cup
Cheddar cheese, finely grated	125 g	4 oz	½ cup
Salt	¼ tsp	¼ tsp	¼ tsp

Beat the butter into the flour with a rotary or electric beater, then beat in the grated cheese and seasonings. Shape the dough into two equal-sized balls with lightly floured hands. Chill for 45 minutes.

On a floured surface, roll out one ball of dough into a rectangle 6 mm/¼ in thick. Leave the other ball chilled. Cut the rolled-out dough into fingers 7–8 cm/3 in long and about 1 cm/½ in wide. Repeat using the remaining dough. Bake at 180°C/350°F/Gas Mark 4 for 15–17 minutes until light gold. Cool on the sheets. Serve cold.

Makes about 5 dozen straws.

Dunkers

 (except cucumber) 3 months

INGREDIENTS

Cauliflower sprigs
Salt
Cucumber
Inner stalks of celery
Fennel stems
Small carrots
Asparagus spears, cooked

Choose from these or other firm 'dippable' vegetables. Add radishes, button mushrooms or olives if you can be bothered to stick wooden toothpicks into them as 'carriers'.

Blanch cauliflower sprigs in boiling salted water for 3–4 minutes. Quarter cucumber lengthways, scrape celery and fennel if needed. Cut cucumber, celery, fennel and carrot into 6 cm/$2\frac{1}{2}$ in lengths. Arrange vegetables in lines or clumps on a big platter with contrasting colours side by side. There's no need to season them if you serve them with any of the following five delicious dips.

Taramasalata

 1 month

INGREDIENTS	Metric	Imperial	American
White bread slices without crusts	12	12	12
Milk	275 ml	$\frac{1}{2}$ pt	$1\frac{1}{4}$ cups
Smoked cod's roe, skinned	175 g	6 oz	6 oz
Onion, skinned and chopped	$\frac{1}{4}$	$\frac{1}{4}$	$\frac{1}{4}$
Juice of 2 lemons			
Oil	225 ml	8 fl oz	1 cup

Soak the bread in the milk. Squeeze it dry. Put it in an electric blender with the smoked roe, onion and lemon juice. Blend until smooth; still blending, trickle in the oil until the mixture becomes smooth and creamy. Refrigerate until well chilled. Serve hot pitta with this dip as well as vegetable Dunkers.

Piccalilli Dip

INGREDIENTS	Metric	Imperial	American
Piccalilli	125 g	4 oz	$\frac{1}{2}$ cup
Natural yoghurt	150 ml	$\frac{1}{4}$ pt	$\frac{2}{3}$ cup
Salt and pepper			

Chop the piccalilli, beat in the yoghurt and season.

Spicy Tomato Dip

 2 months

INGREDIENTS	Metric	Imperial	American
Full-fat soft ('cream') cheese	125 g	4 oz	½ cup
Milk	1 tbsp	1 tbsp	1 tbsp
Tomato chutney	2 tsp	2 tsp	2 tsp
Lemon juice	1 tsp	1 tsp	1 tsp
Tabasco	3–4 drops	3–4 drops	3–4 drops
Salt and black pepper			

Process all the ingredients together in a food processor or blender. Alternatively, beat them thoroughly, using an electric or rotary beater. Adjust the seasoning.

Creamy Onion-Cucumber Dip

2 months (without cucumber)

INGREDIENTS	Metric	Imperial	American
Full-fat soft ('cream') cheese	125 g	4 oz	½ cup
Milk	1 tbsp	1 tbsp	1 tbsp
Cream of Onion Soup Mix	1 tbsp	1 tbsp	1 tbsp
Cucumber, diced	25 mm piece	25 mm piece	1 in piece

Process the cheese, milk and dried soup mix together in a food processor or blender. Alternatively, stir the soup mix with a little of the milk until creamy, then beat in the cheese and remaining milk. Leave the mixture to stand for 15 minutes. Fold in the cucumber.

Blue Cheese Dip

2 weeks

INGREDIENTS	Metric	Imperial	American
Blue cheese, crumbled	75 g	3 oz	½ cup
Cottage cheese	225 g	8 oz	1 cup
Onion juice	½ tsp	½ tsp	½ tsp
Thick fresh or soured cream as needed	4–6 tbsp	4–6 tbsp	4–6 tbsp

Crumble the blue cheese into the cottage cheese, and mix well, adding the onion juice. Add enough cream to give the dip the consistency you prefer.

SALADS

Danish Chef's Salad

INGREDIENTS	Metric	Imperial	American
Cos lettuce	1/2	1/2	1/2
1 medium-sized bunch radishes			
Cucumber	5 cm	2 in	2 in
Onion	1	1	1
Cooked ham	225 g	8 oz	1/2 lb
Danish Blue cheese	125 g	4 oz	2/3 cup
Salt and pepper			
Pinch of dry mustard			
Pinch of caster sugar			
Pure corn oil	4 tbsp	4 tbsp	4 tbsp
White wine vinegar	2 tbsp	2 tbsp	2 tbsp

Prepare and slice the lettuce and radishes, and slice the cucumber. Skin the onion and slice it finely, then separate into rings. Cut the ham into small strips, and the Danish Blue into small cubes. Layer all these ingredients or jumble them lightly in a glass bowl. Put the seasonings in a glass jar with a secure stopper. Add the oil and shake well to blend, then add the vinegar and shake to mix. Shake again and toss lightly with the salad just before serving.

Sunshine Salad

INGREDIENTS	Metric	Imperial	American
Hard-boiled (hard-cooked) eggs	2	2	2
Raw button mushrooms	50 g	2 oz	1/2 cup
Can of sweetcorn, drained	200 g can	7-oz can	7-oz can
Salt and pepper			
Carrots	125 g	4 oz	1/4 lb
Oil or lemon juice			
French mustard	1/2 tsp	1/2 tsp	1/2 tsp
Soured cream	1 tbsp	1 tbsp	1 tbsp
Finely chopped parsley to garnish			

Separate the egg white and yolks. Chop both separately; leave the yolks aside. Chop the mushrooms and mix with the egg whites and drained sweetcorn. Season, and tip into the centre of a large platter. Grate the carrots and mix with a little oil or lemon juice to prevent blackening. Arrange around the sweetcorn mixture. Mix together the mustard, soured cream and chopped egg yolks. Pour this dressing over the corn mixture, and garnish with finely chopped parsley.

Cucumber and Yoghurt Salad

INGREDIENTS

For each person, use:

	Metric	Imperial	American
Fresh mint leaves, finely chopped	1 tsp	1 tsp	1 tsp
Natural yoghurt	1 tbsp	1 tbsp	1 tbsp
Salt and black pepper			
Cucumber piece, unpeeled	5 cm	2 in	2 in

Mix the chopped mint leaves with the yoghurt, and season to taste.
Dice the cucumber, and pour the yoghurt over it. Chill before serving.

Domates Salata

INGREDIENTS

	Metric	Imperial	American
New potatoes, boiled and diced	340 g	12 oz	2 cups
Medium-sized tomatoes skinned, de-seeded and chopped	225 g	8 oz	1 cup
Onion, finely chopped	1	1	1
Black olives, stoned	50 g	2 oz	$\frac{1}{4}$ cup
Mayonnaise	3 tbsp	3 tbsp	3 tbsp
Milk	2 tbsp	2 tbsp	2 tbsp
Black pepper			

Toss all the vegetables together. Mix the mayonnaise with the milk
and pepper, and toss lightly with the vegetables, coating them
evenly. Chill. Use as a side salad.

Californian Fruit Salad

 3 months (using canned fruit, without mayonnaise)

INGREDIENTS

	Metric	Imperial	American
Can of pineapple chunks in natural juice, drained	215 g can	$7\frac{1}{2}$-oz can	$7\frac{1}{2}$-oz can
Can of peach halves in natural juice, drained	215 g can	$7\frac{1}{2}$-oz can	$7\frac{1}{2}$-oz can
OR	**OR**	**OR**	**OR**
Fresh peaches, skinned	3	3	3
Young celery stalks	4	4	4
Flaked almonds	3 tbsp	3 tbsp	3 tbsp
Mayonnaise	2 tbsp	2 tbsp	2 tbsp

Chop the drained fruits and celery. Mix with the almonds and bind
with mayonnaise.

Trader Vic's Salad

INGREDIENTS	Metric	Imperial	American
Frozen peas	225 g	8 oz	1¼ cups
Frozen sweetcorn	225 g	8 oz	1¼ cups
Salt			
Can of pineapple pieces, drained	227 g	8 oz	8 oz
Small sweet red pepper, de-seeded and chopped	1	1	1
Mayonnaise	3 tbsp	3 tbsp	3 tbsp
Single (light) cream	2 tbsp	2 tbsp	2 tbsp
Rind and juice of 1 small lemon			
Paprika			

Blanch the peas and sweetcorn in boiling salted water for 2 minutes. Drain and rinse under a cold tap. Mix the peas and sweetcorn with the pineapple pieces and pepper. Blend the mayonnaise with the cream, lemon rind and juice, and paprika. Toss with the vegetables and chill before serving.

Plain Coleslaw

INGREDIENTS	Metric	Imperial	American
Small white cabbage	½	½	½
Flaked almonds	2½ tbsp	2½ tbsp	2½ tbsp
Raisins (optional)	2 tbsp	2 tbsp	2 tbsp
Mayonnaise	2 tbsp	2 tbsp	2 tbsp
White wine vinegar or lemon juice	2 tsp	2 tsp	2 tsp

Shred the cabbage as finely as possible. Crisp up limp cabbage by standing it in cold water after slicing. Add nuts, and raisins if used, then mix with the mayonnaise and vinegar or lemon juice. Season to taste. Particularly good as a side salad with grills.

Carrot and Orange Salad

❄ 3 months

INGREDIENTS	Metric	Imperial	American
Large carrots, grated	2	2	2
Orange	1	1	1
Ground black pepper			

Grate the carrots coarsely or finely according to taste. Squeeze the juice from the orange and pour it over them. Sprinkle with black pepper. Try with lemon juice for a change.

Pineapple Slaw

INGREDIENTS	Metric	Imperial	American
Firm white cabbage	650 g	1¼ lb	1¼ lb
Small fresh pineapple about 1 kg/2 lb	1	1	1
Walnut halves	75 g	3 oz	½ cup
Sharp dessert apple	1	1	1
Dressing			
Mayonnaise	50 ml	2 fl oz	¼ cup
Natural yoghurt	125 ml	4 fl oz	½ cup
Salt and pepper			
Clear honey	2 tsp	2 tsp	2 tsp
Lemon or orange juice			

Cut out the cabbage stalk and shred the leaves finely. Peel, quarter and core the pineapple, and cut the flesh into small cubes; add any free juice made while cutting it. Peel, quarter and core the apple. Cut the flesh into small cubes, and toss them at once with the pineapple juice and cubes. Mix both fruits and the juice with the cabbage. Reserve 6 or 8 walnut halves for garnishing the salad. Chop and mix in the rest.

Mix thoroughly the mayonnaise and yoghurt for the dressing, stirring until the yoghurt is liquid and smooth. Add a scrap of seasoning. Stir in the honey, then sharpen with 5 ml/1 tsp juice or to taste, depending on the flavour of the yoghurt. Toss the slaw with with the dressing, cover and refrigerate. Toss again and garnish just before serving.

Potato and Bacon Salad

 2 weeks (without dressing)

INGREDIENTS	Metric	Imperial	American
Bacon rashers (strips) without rind	4	4	4
Cheddar or other hard cheese	75 g	3 oz	¾ cup
Cocktail gherkins	2	2	2
Small onion or medium-sized shallot	1	1	1
Boiled potatoes, cooled and diced	350 g	12 oz	¾ lb
Finely chopped parsley	1 tsp	1 tsp	1 tsp
Oil and vinegar dressing (page 38)	1 tbsp	1 tbsp	1 tbsp

Grill the bacon until crisp, then dice or chop it. While it cools, dice the cheese and chop the gherkins and onion finely. Mix these ingredients with the potatoes and parsley. Sprinkle with the dressing.

DRESSINGS

Basic Oil and Vinegar Dressing

INGREDIENTS

	Metric	Imperial	American
Oil	2 tbsp	2 tbsp	2 tbsp
Vinegar (usually white wine vinegar)	1 tbsp	1 tbsp	1 tbsp
Salt and freshly ground black pepper			

The quantities will obviously depend on the quantity of salad, but the 2: 1 ratio is constant. This is so for all the oil-based dressings given here.

VARIATIONS

Add one of the following:
2 tsp mixed chopped parsley, marjoram and thyme.
2 tsp mixed chopped parsley, gherkin and olives.
1 tsp mixed chopped chives and tarragon plus $\frac{1}{2}$ tsp mustard.
$\frac{1}{2}$ tsp Worcestershire sauce and 1 tsp chopped onion.
1 tsp chopped mint.
1 tsp drained and chopped anchovies.
1 tbsp crumbled blue cheese.
$\frac{1}{2}$ tsp curry powder plus 1 sieved hard-boiled (hard-cooked) egg
    yolk.
Lemon juice instead of vinegar.

Basic Mayonnaise

INGREDIENTS

	Metric	Imperial	American
Egg yolk	1	1	1
Dry mustard	$\frac{1}{2}$ tsp	$\frac{1}{2}$ tsp	$\frac{1}{2}$ tsp
Sugar	$\frac{1}{2}$ tsp	$\frac{1}{2}$ tsp	$\frac{1}{2}$ tsp
Oil	150 ml	$\frac{1}{4}$ pt	$\frac{5}{8}$ cup
White wine vinegar	1 tbsp	1 tbsp	1 tbsp

Mix the egg yolk with the mustard and sugar, and whisk (beat) well. Add the oil drop by drop, whisking (beating) all the time. Finally stir in the vinegar drop by drop.

VARIATIONS

Add one of the following flavourings:
2 tsp chopped capers and chopped pimento
4 tbsp whipped cream
2 tsp chopped chives and parsley
1 tsp tomato ketchup (catsup) and paprika pepper
1 tbsp crumbled blue cheese

Basic Vinaigrette Dressing

INGREDIENTS	Metric	Imperial	American
Oil	2 tbsp	2 tbsp	2 tbsp
White wine vinegar	1 tbsp	1 tbsp	1 tbsp
Dry mustard	½ tsp	½ tsp	½ tsp
Sugar	¼ tsp	¼ tsp	¼ tsp
Chopped onion	1 tsp	1 tsp	1 tsp
Chopped parsley	1 tsp	1 tsp	1 tsp

Mix well together before pouring over the salad.

Basic French Dressing

INGREDIENTS	Metric	Imperial	American
Oil	2 tbsp	2 tbsp	2 tbsp
Vinegar	1 tbsp	1 tbsp	1 tbsp
Mustard	½ tsp	½ tsp	½ tsp
Sugar	¼ tsp	¼ tsp	¼ tsp
Salt and black pepper			

Mix well together with a fork before pouring over the salad. Different flavours can be obtained by using English, French, Dijon, German or American mustard.

Bouquet Dressing

INGREDIENTS	Metric	Imperial	American
Chopped fresh chervil	½ tsp	½ tsp	½ tsp
Chopped chives	1 tsp	1 tsp	1 tsp
Chopped parsley	1 tbsp	1 tbsp	1 tbsp
French mustard	1 tsp	1 tsp	1 tsp
Salt	½ tsp	½ tsp	½ tsp
Black pepper	¼ tsp	¼ tsp	¼ tsp
Garlic clove, crushed (minced)	1	1	1
Olive oil	225 ml	8 fl oz	1 cup
Tarragon vinegar	4 tbsp	4 tbsp	4 tbsp
Lemon juice	2 tsp	2 tsp	2 tsp

Mix the chervil, chives, parsley, mustard, salt, pepper and garlic in a small bowl, using a wooden spoon. Slowly, stir in 3 tbsp of the oil. Pour the mixture into a clean jar with a screw-top lid or firm stopper. Add the remaining oil, the vinegar and lemon juice. Close the jar securely, and shake vigorously for 1 minute.

Use as required, and store the rest in the refrigerator until needed. Use within 1 week.

Makes about 275 ml/½ pt/1¼ cups.

Soured Cream Dressing

INGREDIENTS

	Metric	Imperial	American
Hard-boiled (hard-cooked) egg yolks	2	2	2
Soured cream	125 ml	4 fl oz	$\frac{1}{2}$ cup
A few drops of tarragon vinegar			
Salt and pepper			

Sieve the egg yolks and mix to a smooth paste with a little of the cream. Add the remaining cream, blending it in smoothly. Flavour with the vinegar, and season to taste.

Makes about 125 ml/4 fl oz/$\frac{1}{2}$ cup.

Honey Dressing

INGREDIENTS

	Metric	Imperial	American
Clear honey	2 tbsp	2 tbsp	2 tbsp
Lemon juice	4 tbsp	4 tbsp	4 tbsp
Olive oil	6 tbsp	6 tbsp	6 tbsp
French mustard	$\frac{1}{2}$ tsp	$\frac{1}{2}$ tsp	$\frac{1}{2}$ tsp
Salt	$\frac{1}{4}$ tsp	$\frac{1}{4}$ tsp	$\frac{1}{4}$ tsp
Black pepper	$\frac{1}{8}$ tsp	$\frac{1}{8}$ tsp	$\frac{1}{8}$ tsp

In a small mixing bowl or jug, beat all the ingredients together with a fork or wire whisk until well blended. Alternatively, put them all into a screw-topped jar, close it securely, and shake vigorously for 10 seconds. Use as required.

Makes about 200 ml/7 fl oz/1 cup minus 2 tbsp.

Blue Cheese Dressing

INGREDIENTS

	Metric	Imperial	American
Blue cheese (Roquefort, Danish Blue, etc.)	50 g	2 oz	$\frac{1}{4}$ cup
Natural yoghurt	125 ml	4 fl oz	$\frac{1}{2}$ cup
Strained lemon juice	1 tsp	1 tsp	1 tsp
A few drops of clear honey (optional)			

Crumble the cheese finely. Put all the ingredients in a food processor and blend until smooth. Use cold over hot vegetables such as cauliflower or beetroot, or over a root vegetable salad or slaw.

Makes 6 fl oz/175 ml/$\frac{3}{4}$ cup dressing.

Two-Way Yoghurt Dressing

INGREDIENTS	Metric	Imperial	American
First Dressing			
Natural yoghurt	125 ml	4 fl oz	½ cup
Soured cream	2 tbsp	2 tbsp	2 tbsp
Mixed English mustard	¼ tsp	¼ tsp	¼ tsp
Lemon juice	1 tbsp	1 tbsp	1 tbsp
Salt and pepper			
Second dressing			
Natural yoghurt	75 ml	3 fl oz	⅓ cup
Whipping or single cream	4 tbsp	4 tbsp	4 tbsp
Dijon mustard	1 tbsp	1 tbsp	1 tbsp
Salt and pepper if needed			

Stir the yoghurt until smooth. Stir in the remaining ingredients for the dressing you choose. Taste and adjust the seasoning if needed. Cover and chill until needed. The dressing should thicken but not be solid.

Makes 150 ml/¼ pt/⅔ cup dressing.

You could make the second dressing with mayonnaise instead of yoghurt and add 2 tsp lemon juice for extra tang. This version is called Creamy Mustard Mayonnaise.

Coleslaw Dressing

INGREDIENTS	Metric	Imperial	American
Mayonnaise	275 ml	½ pt	1¼ cups
Natural yoghurt	4 tbsp	4 tbsp	4 tbsp
Sugar	1 tsp	1 tsp	1 tsp
Salt	½ tsp	½ tsp	½ tsp
Finely grated (minced) onion	1 tbsp	1 tbsp	1 tbsp
Finely chopped celery	1 tbsp	1 tbsp	1 tbsp

Blend the mayonnaise and yoghurt with a wooden spoon until smooth. Add the remaining ingredients, and beat for 1 minute. Use at once.

Makes 350 ml/12 fl oz/1½ cups.

DESSERTS

Fresh fruit is one of the best desserts to follow barbecued food; but fruit/desserts grilled on the barbecue, and for a party a light but fancy, frivolous dessert dish will also add glamour to the occasion.

Barbados Oranges

 6 months (before grilling)

INGREDIENTS	Metric	Imperial	American
Large oranges	4	4	4
Soft brown sugar	4 tbsp	4 tbsp	4 tbsp
Ground cinnamon			
Rum	4 tbsp	4 tbsp	4 tbsp
Butter	4 tsp	4 tsp	4 tsp
Whipped cream			

Have ready 4 doubled squares of aluminium oil. Peel the oranges, removing any pith, and divide each into segments, keeping the oranges separate. Place the segments of each orange on a separate piece of foil. Sprinkle each portion with 1 tbsp sugar, a pinch of ground cinnamon and 1 tbsp rum. Dot each with 1 tsp butter. Fold foil over the fruit segments to enclose them. Barbecue on the grill for 15–20 minutes. Serve hot, with whipped cream.

Golden Grilled Peaches

 3 months (before grilling)

INGREDIENTS	Metric	Imperial	American
1 medium can peach halves in syrup	425 g can	15 oz can	15 oz can
(6–8 halves)			
1 small pkt Philadelphia soft cheese	75 g pkt	3 oz pkt	3 oz pkt
Finely chopped walnut pieces	1 tbsp	1 tbsp	1 tbsp
Syrup from can of peaches	1 tbsp	1 tbsp	1 tbsp
Demerara (golden crystal) sugar			

Drain the peach halves, reserving the syrup. Mash the cheese and walnuts in a small bowl with 1 tbsp of the syrup to moisten it. Fill equal quantities into the hollows in the peaches. Place the peaches cut side up on a small heavy baking sheet or tripled thickness of stout foil, well greased. Sprinkle the cheese filling with sugar. Place on medium heat on the barbecue grill until the sugar begins to melt.

Ginger and Lemon Cheesecake

 2 months

INGREDIENTS	Metric	Imperial	American
Gingernut biscuits (hard cookies)	175 g	6 oz	6 oz
Butter or margarine	50 g	2 oz	$\frac{1}{4}$ cup
Gelatine	15 g	$\frac{1}{2}$ oz	1 sachet
Water	2 tbsp	2 tbsp	2 tbsp
Lemons	2	2	2
Cottage cheese	125 g	4 oz	$\frac{1}{4}$ lb
Full fat soft, cream, cheese	125 g	4 oz	$\frac{1}{4}$ lb
Caster (granulated) sugar	50 g	2 oz	$\frac{1}{4}$ cup
Natural yoghurt	150 ml	$\frac{1}{4}$ pt	$\frac{2}{3}$ cup
Double (heavy) cream	150 ml	$\frac{1}{4}$ pt	$\frac{2}{3}$ cup

Break up the biscuits (cookies) and process in a food processor or blender, or put in a plastic bag and crush with a rolling pin. Tip the crumbs into a bowl. Melt the fat and add to the crumbs. Stir well, then press into the base of a 20 cm/8 in flan ring on a platter. Chill.

Place the gelatine in a small bowl with the water, and stand in a pan of water. Heat gently until the gelatine dissolves.

Use a potato peeler to pare 2–3 thin strips of lemon rind from 1 lemon. Grate the remaining rind of both lemons. Cut the lemons into quarters, remove the pips and skin, and purée the flesh. Do this by processing in a blender for 10–15 seconds or by rubbing hard through a metal sieve. Add the cottage cheese and the soft cheese cut into pieces. Blend for 10–15 seconds or beat hard until all are mixed thoroughly. Add the grated lemon rind, caster sugar, yoghurt and cream. Blend or beat again. Pour in the gelatine mixture and blend or beat quickly to prevent lumps forming. Pour into the crumb flan case and leave in the fridge for 1 hour to set. Decorate with lemon rind cut into thin strips and with extra cream if required.

Pineapple Ice Cream Pie

 2 months (without garnish)

INGREDIENTS	Metric	Imperial	American
Digestive (sweetmeal) biscuits	125 g	4 oz	$\frac{1}{4}$ lb
Butter or margarine	50 g	2 oz	$\frac{1}{4}$ cup
Pineapple pieces in natural juice	275 g can	10 oz can	10 oz can
Cornflour	1 tsp	1 tsp	1 tsp
Lemon	$\frac{1}{2}$	$\frac{1}{2}$	$\frac{1}{2}$
Honey	1 tsp	1 tsp	1 tsp
Soft scoop ice cream	1 l	$1\frac{3}{4}$ pt	$4\frac{1}{3}$ cups
Almonds	25 g	1 oz	1 oz

Break up the biscuits, then crush them in a blender in batches or place them in a bag and crush with a rolling pin. Add the melted butter or margarine and press into a 20 cm/8 in flan ring. Place in the fridge.

Drain the juice from the can of pineapple. Blend the cornflour with a little of the juice, then heat the rest of the juice with the juice of ½ lemon and 1 tsp of honey. Add the hot liquid to the cornflour mixture and return to the pan over a low heat to thicken. Allow to cool. Reserve a few pieces for decoration, then purée the remaining pineapple pieces in a blender or rub through a sieve and add to the sauce.

Place scoops of the ice cream in the biscuit base, arranging them round and into a pyramid shape. Pour the pineapple sauce over the ice cream. Place in the freezer for 20–30 minutes. Remove, sprinkle with nuts and decorate with the reserved pineapple pieces. Serve immediately.

Blackberry Soufflé

3 months (in the dish)

INGREDIENTS	Metric	Imperial	American
Blackberries	450 g	1 lb	1 lb
Water	75 ml	5 tbsp	5 tbsp
Eggs	4	4	4
Caster sugar	125 g	4 oz	½ cup
Gelatine	15 g	½ oz	1 sachet
Whipping cream	275 ml	½ pt	1¼ cups

Reserve a few of the blackberries for decoration. Cook the remaining blackberries in water for 10 minutes over a gentle heat. Purée in a blender in batches or rub through a sieve.

Separate the eggs. Place the yolks in a large bowl with the caster sugar and whisk (beat) over a pan of hot water until thick and creamy. Remove from the heat and whisk until cool. Dissolve the gelatine in a small bowl in 3 tbsp of water and stand over hot water to melt.

Whisk the egg whites until stiff. Whisk half the cream until it forms soft peaks. Add the melted gelatine to the fruit purée, then fold this into the egg yolk mixture. Carefully fold in the whipped cream and then the egg whites. Make a collar of greaseproof paper round an 18 cm/7 in soufflé dish. Pour the mixture into the dish and leave to set in the fridge for 5–6 hours or overnight.

Remove the greaseproof band, whisk the remaining cream and pipe in rosettes on top. Decorate with a few reserved blackberries.

This can also be made with other soft fruits such as raspberries, strawberries etc.

DRINKS

Keep drinks simple – and plentiful. Use big mugs rather than cups, and plastic glasses for soft drinks because people tend to leave them around on the ground. As a beverage, most people now prefer coffee to tea. As for other drinks, beer is always popular with men, certainly at an informal barbecue, although a simple choice of red and white wine always makes summer drinking a pleasure. Keep it chilled 'on site' in a bucket or tin bath of broken or dry ice.

If you have a barman to serve it, your guests will enjoy a cold fruit punch, or, for a cold-weather barbecue mulled ale or cider.

Always serve at least one long soft drink such as Spiced Tomato Juice, and have plenty of fruit juices for children.

Spiced Tomato Juice

3 months

INGREDIENTS	Metric	Imperial	American
Whole cloves	4	4	4
Celery tops with leaves	3	3	3
Tomato juice	750 ml	1¼ pt	3 cups
Water	225 ml	8 fl oz	1 cup
Granulated sugar	1 tbsp	1 tbsp	1 tbsp
Worcestershire sauce	1 tsp	1 tsp	1 tsp
Pinch of cayenne pepper			
Salt	¼ tsp	¼ tsp	¼ tsp
Lemon juice	2 tsp	2 tsp	2 tsp

Tie the cloves and celery tops in a piece of cloth. Put all the ingredients in a saucepan and simmer for 20 minutes uncovered. Strain into a jug, cool and chill. Can be stored in the refrigerator in a jar with a well-fitting lid for 3–4 days.

Port-of-Call Party Punch

 3 months (without soda water)

INGREDIENTS	Metric	Imperial	American
Burgundy wine	1.1 l	1 qrt	5 cups
Port wine	125 ml	4 fl oz	½ cup
Cherry brandy	50 ml	2 fl oz	¼ cup
Juice of 1½ lemons			
Juice of 3 oranges			
Caster sugar	50 g	2 oz	¼ cup
Soda water	1.1 l	1 qrt	5 cups
Fresh fruit			

Mix all the ingredients except the sugar and soda water. Add most or all of the sugar to suit your taste; stir it until it dissolves. Pour the mixture over a large block of ice in a punch bowl. Just before serving, add the soda water.
    Serves 6–8.

Mulled Cider

 2 months (before heating)

INGREDIENTS	Metric	Imperial	American
Medium dry cider (alcoholic)	1.1 l	1 qrt	2½ pt
Muscovado sugar	40 g	1½ oz	8 tsp
Pinch of salt			
Whole cloves	4	4	4
Piece of cinnamon stick 5 cm/2 in long			
Allspice berries	4	4	4
Strip of orange peel			

Put the cider, sugar and salt in a saucepan. Tie the spices loosely in a piece of cloth and add it. Bring gently to the boil, cover and simmer for 12–15 minutes. Serve hot in mugs.

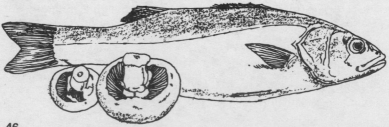

ON THE BARBECUE

FLAVOURING YOUR FOOD

First-class meat has a fine flavour of its own but herbs, spices and seasonings can highlight it and give it new interest. They can be rubbed into the meat itself, be added to a marinade, baste or sauce, or can be put on the fire in the form of burning woods and herbs.

You can use any herbs or spices which appeal to you. There are no fixed rules as to which you should use although some herbs are traditional with particular meat dishes. Look at the recipes in the following sections as a guide to suitable choices.

Always use fresh herbs if you can, or good quality dried herbs in jars from a store with a quick turnover.

Besides single herbs and spices, most large firms supply ready-mixed combinations: lemon and pepper seasoning for instance, and various barbecue seasonings. Try them, cautiously, on one small item at first. You may find you like them or that you prefer your own individual 'mixes'.

The same goes for the various marinade and barbecue sauce 'mixes' on the market. If you use them, try adding a touch of your own such as a spoonful of wine or a scrap of squeezed garlic.

If you decide to try barbecue-burning woods and herbs, remember that they will scent the whole fire, so be cautious if you have various different meats and fish items on the grill. You don't want them all to have the same character. If you are barbecuing just one or two different foods, these mixtures can be a delight sending their fragrant aroma into the air as well as scenting the food itself. They are distributed by Living Flair Ltd., 103 Brunel Road, Earlstrees Industrial Estate, Corby, Northants.

Get the most out of the simplest spices. Sea salt has more vigour than table salt, the slightly unusual spicy note of mignonette pepper can be delicious, and there are now excellent ready-mixed herb and spice mustards available in most supermarkets.

BEEF

BEEF BASICS

Basic Recipe: Hamburgers

A basic hamburger recipe is a 'must' in your barbecue cooking because you can liven it up in any number of ways.

Try crusty-topped rolls, for instance, or toasted English muffins instead of buns. Wholemeal rolls have a delicious nutty flavour, especially good with cheeseburgers. Offer a selection of relishes, or provide different sauces such as Home-Made Mayonnaise (page 38), or Blue Cheese Dressing (page 40) for the more venturesome.

Do you want a quick, simple supper? Try mushroom 'burgers: hamburgers on toasted buns with a spoonful of undiluted condensed mushroom soup ladled over each – or you might experiment with slices of processed cheese and chopped canned pineapple. They transform ordinary patties into South Sea treats.

Good hamburgers depend on the quality of the minced (ground) beef you use. When you buy fresh meat, you may find more than one grade of mince (ground beef) on sale, each containing a different amount of fat – usually between 15 and 30 per cent. The lean meat may differ in quality too, and it may be finely or coarsely minced (ground). Good quality meat obviously costs more than meat from a cheaper cut, so your pocket as well as your preference for fine or coarse-cut meat may decide which you buy. Recipes in this book simply call for lean minced (ground) beef.

INGREDIENTS	Metric	Imperial	American
Lean minced (ground) beef	1.4 kg	3 lb	3 lb
Salt and pepper			
Soft-topped round rolls (buns), split			
for toasting	8	8	8
Butter (optional)			

Shape the meat into 8 equal-sized round patties. Since the loss of fat while cooking makes them shrink a little, flatten the patties with your palm if necessary to make them slightly larger than the rolls.

Place the patties on a lightly greased grill 10–15 cm/4–6 in above a solid bed of well-heated coals; you should only be able to hold your hand at meat level for 2 seconds before pulling it away. Cook, turning once with a slice, for 3–4 minutes on each side if you like rare 'burgers or for 5–6 minutes for well-done meat. Place rolls, cut side down, around the edge of the grill to toast while cooking the 'burgers, or butter them and warm them on the grill, cut side up. Season the 'burgers with salt and pepper when done, and sandwich them in the rolls.

Serves 8.

Basic Recipe:Grilled Steak

Most barbecue cooks think of steak when anyone mentions having beef on the menu. Fillet, rump, sirloin, Porterhouse – whatever type of steak you choose, see that it's between 2.5 and 5 cm/1 and 2 in thick.

Don't season steak before cooking; it toughens the fibres. Turn it once only while cooking, and take care not to puncture it when doing so; piercing it with a fork will make the meat juices drip out and fall into the fire, causing flare-ups. Turn it with tongs or a spatula or slice. Salt it after cooking.

INGREDIENTS	Metric	Imperial	American
Individual steaks, 275–400 g/10–14 oz each, cut 2.5–5 cm/1–2 in thick	6–8	6–8	6–8
Baste (see page 00), optional			
Salt and pepper			
Savoury butter (see page 20), optional			

Snip any fat around the edges of the steaks at equal intervals to prevent it curling during cooking. Snip it just to where the fat meets the flesh. Place the steaks on a lightly greased grill, 10–15 cm/4–6 in above the well-heated coals, which should be as hot as for hamburgers. Cook steaks for 5–8 minutes on each side if wanted rare, 7–10 minutes if wanted well done. Transfer steaks to a serving platter, and season. Check doneness by scoring the tops deeply in a criss-cross pattern 5 or 6 times. If you wish, spread with about 2 tbsp savoury butter (page 20).

Serves 6–8.

Note
If you prefer, cook a single large steak weighing about 1.4 kg/3 lb, and cut 5 cm/2 in thick. Cook for 12–15 min per side for rare steak. If using a covered grill, reduce the total time by 5 minutes.

Basic Recipe: Roast Beef on a Covered Grill

Any 1.4–2.3 kg/3–5 lb piece of boneless beef will cook in under 2 hours on a covered grill, and will be tastier than when oven-roasted. This recipe calls for a rolled rib roast but other good cuts cook equally well. For less tender cuts such as silverside (bottom round), it's wise to marinate the meat before cooking (see page 18).

INGREDIENTS	Metric	Imperial	American
Herb-wine marinade (page 19)			
Rolled rib roast	1.4–2.3 kg	3–5 lb	3–5 lb

Prepare the marinade. Place the prepared joint in a non-metallic bowl which fits it closely, or in a plastic bag in a shallow bowl or dish. Pour the marinade over the meat. Cover the bowl, or twist and tie the bag to close it. Refrigerate until next day, turning the meat over occasionally, to make sure the meat soaks into it all over.

Bank the fire on each side of the fire-bowl, and place a metal drip-pan in the centre. Place the grill 10–15 cm/4–6 in above the drip-pan, and grease it lightly. Remove the meat from the marinade, and drain it briefly; reserve the marinade. Insert a meat thermometer into the thickest part of the meat. Place the meat on the grill, directly over the drip-pan. Cover the barbecue, and adjust the dampers according to the manufacturer's directions. Cook, basting occasionally with reserved marinade, for 1½ hours for rare beef or until the meat thermometer registers 60–71°C/140–160°F. Make sure you maintain a constant temperature. When the roast is ready, let it stand for about 20 minutes to firm up. Then carve it in thin slices. Serves 6–10, depending on size of joint.

OTHER BEEF RECIPES

Flamed Pepper Steak

Hot, garlic-scented tomato slices garnish this classic pepper steak. Flaming brandy is spooned over the steak just before serving.

INGREDIENTS

	Metric	Imperial	American
Coarsely ground black pepper	1 tsp	1 tsp	1 tsp
Sirloin (club) steaks, cut 2.5 cm/1 in thick	4	4	4
Butter or margarine	3 tbsp	3 tbsp	3 tbsp
Large firm tomatoes	2	2	2
Dried basil	$\frac{1}{8}$ tsp	$\frac{1}{8}$ tsp	$\frac{1}{2}$ tsp
Garlic salt	$\frac{1}{8}$ tsp	$\frac{1}{8}$ tsp	$\frac{1}{8}$ tsp
Brandy	4 tbsp	4 tbsp	4 tbsp

Sprinkle the pepper over both sides of the steaks; press and force it into the surfaces. Leave the steaks to stand for 30 minutes.

Slice the tomatoes about 1 cm/$\frac{1}{2}$ in thick. Melt the butter in a frying pan, and cook the tomatoes until just heated through. Transfer to a platter, season with basil and garlic salt and keep warm.

Place the steaks on the lightly greased grill 10–15 cm/4–6 in above the coals. Cook, turning once, for 5 minutes on each side for rare steaks, or until done as you prefer when scored (see page 49). Arrange the steaks on a warmed platter with the tomato slices for formal serving. Ignite the brandy, and tip a spoonful over each steak before serving.

Steak with Rosemary

Flavoured just with fresh rosemary, a large thick slice of first-class beef grilled on a barbecue is both simple and special.

INGREDIENTS

	Metric	Imperial	American
Fresh rosemary leaves	2 tbsp	2 tbsp	2 tbsp
OR	OR	OR	OR
Dried rosemary leaves	2 tsp	2 tsp	2 tsp
Single large slice of beef topside (rump roast), weight about 1.8 kg/4 lb, cut 5 cm/2 in thick	1	1	1
Salt and pepper			

Press the rosemary leaves firmly onto both sides of the meat. Place the steak on a lightly greased grill, 10–15 cm/4–6 in above the coals. If using a covered grill, put on the cover and adjust the dampers as the manufacturer's leaflet directs. Cook, turning once, for about 15 minutes on each side for rare steaks or until done as you prefer. Sprinkle with salt and pepper, and carve the meat across the grain in thin slanting slices.

Serves 6–8.

Whole Fillet and Blue Cheese

A whole beef fillet is a luxury dish, still more so when cooked quickly and served with a tangy blue cheese butter.

INGREDIENTS	Metric	Imperial	American
Butter or margarine, softened	225 g	8 oz	1 cup
Blue cheese without rind	125 g	4 oz	½ cup
Chopped chives or spring onion (scallion) tops	1 tbsp	1 tbsp	1 tbsp
Finely chopped parsley			
Beef fillet, weighing 1.8–2.3 kg/4–5 lb	1	1	1
Salad oil			
Watercress			

Blend the butter or margarine and cheese together until smooth, and mix in the chives or onion tops. Shape into a log, roll in parsley, and wrap in greaseproof (waxed) paper. Chill until firm.

Place the fillet on a lightly greased grill 10–15 cm/4–6 in above hot coals. Cook, turning and brushing with oil, for about 30 minutes for rare steak or until done as you prefer when scored (see page 49). Unwrap the butter, and put it on a bed of watercress. Cut the meat in thin slices, and offer pats of the butter with it.

Serves 8–10.

A-Me'Huat
(Beef Kebabs)

INGREDIENTS	Metric	Imperial	American
Good roasting beef	450 g	1 lb	1 lb
Vinegar	1 tbsp	1 tbsp	1 tbsp
Ground ginger	1 tbsp	1 tbsp	1 tbsp
Turmeric	¼ tsp	¼ tsp	¼ tsp
Ground coriander	1 tsp	1 tsp	1 tsp
Cumin seeds	¼ tsp	¼ tsp	¼ tsp
Soured milk	3 tbsp	3 tbsp	3 tbsp
Salt	1½ tsp	1½ tsp	1½ tsp
Butter, melted	3 tbsp	3 tbsp	3 tbsp

Cut the meat into 2.5 cm/1 in cubes. Put them in a bowl and sprinkle with the vinegar. Mix the spices together, add the soured milk and salt and pour the mixture over the beef. Leave to stand for 30 minutes. Thread 3 or 4 beef cubes on each of 8 small skewers. Brush with butter. Cook on the barbecue, turning 2–3 times, for 6–7 minutes for rare meat, 10–12 minutes if liked well done. Baste with butter while cooking. Serve 2 small skewers to each person with Pineapple Slaw (page 37) and with Cucumber and Yoghurt Salad (page 35), or with Yellow Rice (page 92) and just one salad.

Mustard-Sauced Steak

When the meat is almost ready, you mix the sauce in a shallow dish in which you can carve the meat. As you slice the meat, its juices blend into the sauce. Swirl each slice in the sauce as you serve it.

INGREDIENTS	Metric	Imperial	American
Large rump steak(s) or slice(s) of topside (top sirloin or top round steak) without bone, 5–8 cm/2–3 in thick	1.8–2.3 kg	4–5 lb	4–5 lb
Garlic clove	1	1	1
Dry vermouth or dry white wine	50 ml	2 fl oz	$\frac{1}{4}$ cup
Dijon mustard	1 tbsp	1 tbsp	1 tbsp
Worcestershire sauce	$\frac{1}{4}$ tsp	$\frac{1}{4}$ tsp	$\frac{1}{4}$ tsp
Powdered dried rosemary, dried basil leaves, oregano leaves and tarragon leaves	$\frac{1}{8}$ tsp each	$\frac{1}{8}$ tsp each	$\frac{1}{8}$ tsp each
Salt and pepper			

Place the meat on the lightly greased grill 10–15 cm/4–6 in above the coals. Cook, turning once, for about 15 minutes on each side for rare meat or until done as you prefer after scoring (see page 49).

When the meat is almost ready, mix the sauce in a shallow dish suitable for carving in. Crush or squeeze (press) the garlic into the dish. Stir in the wine, mustard and Worcestershire sauce. Sprinkle the dried herb leaves on top, and stir round again. Put in the hot meat, and turn it over in the sauce. Season it to taste. Then slice it thinly. Swirl each slice in the sauce as you serve it.

Serves 8–10.

Note
For fewer people, use a smaller quantity of meat but the same amount of sauce.

Beef with Orange Slices

This popular Brazilian combination consists of beef marinated in orange juice and served with fresh orange slices.

INGREDIENTS	Metric	Imperial	American
Grilling beef cut weighing about 700 g/1½ lb, not more than 2.5 cm/1 in thick	1	1	1
Orange juice	125 ml	4 fl oz	½ cup
Dried onion flakes	2 tbsp	2 tbsp	2 tbsp
Garlic cloves, finely chopped or squeezed (minced or pressed)	2	2	2
Black pepper	¼ tsp	¼ tsp	¼ tsp
Salad oil	3 tbsp	3 tbsp	3 tbsp
Red wine vinegar	2 tbsp	2 tbsp	2 tbsp
Ground cumin	¾ tsp	¾ tsp	¾ tsp
Large oranges, peeled and sliced	2 or 3	2 or 3	2 or 3

Beat the meat out thoroughly if required. Trim off any excess fat. Mix together the orange juice, onion flakes, garlic, oil, vinegar and cumin. Pour this marinade over the meat (see page 18 for method); cover and refrigerate, turning the meat over occasionally, for 24 hours.

Drain the meat over the marinade; keep the marinade. Place the meat on a lightly greased grill, 10–15 cm/4–6 in above the coals. Cook, turning once and basting several times with the marinade, for 5–7 minutes on each side for medium-rare meat or until done as you prefer after scoring (see page 49).

To serve, cut the meat in thin slanting slices across the grain. Garnish with orange slices.

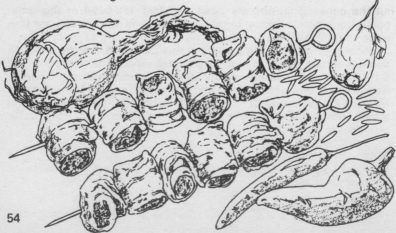

LAMB

LAMB BASICS

Basic Recipe: Lamb Shish Kebab

Shish-kebabs and similar small pieces of lamb barbecued on skewers are standard dishes in many countries. Often, they are spiced or marinated first, and pieces of vegetables or fruit are alternated with the pieces of meat or minced (ground) meatballs.

This basic recipe for skewer-cooked lamb calls for 3 cm/1½-in cubes of lean meat (shoulder or leg) marinated for 2–4 hours, then grilled quickly until browned on all sides. Cooking times for smaller cubes are given at the end of the recipe. You can add pieces of vegetables or fruit alternately with the meat cubes if you like.

The simple marinade given here is based on lemon juice and olive oil with various seasonings.

INGREDIENTS	Metric	Imperial	American
Boneless lean lamb (shoulder or leg)			
cut into 3 cm/1½ in cubes	900 g	2 lb	2 lb
Olive oil or salad oil	65 ml	2½ fl oz	⅓ cup
Lemon juice	3 tbsp	3 tbsp	3 tbsp
Large onion, finely chopped	1	1	1
Bay leaves	2	2	2
Oregano leaves	2 tsp	2 tsp	2 tsp
Black pepper	½ tsp	½ tsp	½ tsp

Put the cubes of lamb in a bowl. In a second bowl or jug, mix together all the remaining ingredients. Pour the marinade over the lamb, and marinate for 2–4 hours.

Drain the lamb cubes in a sieve over the marinade; reserve it. Divide the meat cubes equally between sturdy metal skewers.

Place the lightly greased grill 10–15 cm/4–6 in above the coals. Cook, turning and basting with marinade for 20–25 minutes or until the lamb is well browned on all sides but still slightly pink in the middle when cut through. For 2 cm/¾ in cubes, cook for 12–15 minutes, and for 2.5 cm/1 in cubes, cook 15–20 minutes.

Serves 6.

Basic Recipe: Leg of Lamb on a Covered Grill

If you wish, you can marinate the joint in an onion-flavoured marinade before cooking it, using the mixture below. Marinate the joint for at least 8 hours, preferably overnight. Alternatively baste the meat while cooking with one of the bastes on page 22. Use a meat thermometer if possible.

INGREDIENTS	Metric	Imperial	American
Leg of lamb, bone in, weight about			
2.7 kg/6 lb	*1*	*1*	*1*
Onion-flavoured marinade			
(optional)			
Medium onions, thinly sliced	*2*	*2*	*2*
Black pepper	*½ tsp*	*½ tsp*	*½ tsp*
Sherry or orange juice	*125 ml*	*4 fl oz*	*½ cup*
Olive oil	*2 tbsp*	*2 tbsp*	*2 tbsp*
Oregano leaves	*1 tsp*	*1 tsp*	*1 tsp*
Dried savory leaves	*½ tsp*	*½ tsp*	*½ tsp*

If using the onion-flavoured marinade, mix all the ingredients together and marinate the joint overnight in a shallow dish or plastic bag (see page 18 for method).

Bank the fire on each side of the fire-bowl, and place a metal drip-tray in the centre. Place the grill 10–15 cm/4–6 in above the drip-tray; grease it lightly.

If marinated, drain the joint over the marinade; keep the marinade for basting. If the meat has not been marinated, have ready one of the bastes on page 22. Place the joint on the grill directly over the drip-tray. Cover the barbecue and adjust the dampers according to the manufacturer's directions.

Cook, basting occasionally, for about 2 hours, or until a meat thermometer inserted into the thickest part of the meat registers 63°C/145°F for rare meat, 71°C/160°F for medium-done meat. Maintain a constant temperature.

Serves about 8.

Basic Recipe: Spit-Roasted Leg of Lamb

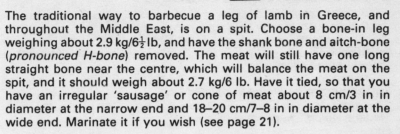

The traditional way to barbecue a leg of lamb in Greece, and throughout the Middle East, is on a spit. Choose a bone-in leg weighing about 2.9 kg/6½ lb, and have the shank bone and aitch-bone (*pronounced H-bone*) removed. The meat will still have one long straight bone near the centre, which will balance the meat on the spit, and it should weigh about 2.7 kg/6 lb. Have it tied, so that you have an irregular 'sausage' or cone of meat about 8 cm/3 in in diameter at the narrow end and 18–20 cm/7–8 in in diameter at the wide end. Marinate it if you wish (see page 21).

INGREDIENTS	Metric	Imperial	American
Leg of lamb as described above	2.7 kg	6 lb	6 lb
Marinade (optional)			
Baste (see page 22)			

Run the spit of a rotisserie attachment through the joint, parallel and close to the bone. Secure it with spit forks (part of the attachment). Test the spit for balance by picking up the spit at both ends, and rotating it with the fingers of one hand while it rests on the palm of the other. If one side of the meat 'drags' seriously, so that when roasting, it will always be facing the fire, re-position it or add a counterbalancing weight on the lighter side. (A slight tendency to spin round doesn't matter; the motor will overcome it.) When the joint is properly balanced, tighten the spit forks to prevent them working loose during cooking.

Make the fire along the back of a square or oblong barbecue, or parallel with the spit-holder in a round fire-bowl. The fire should extend 8–10 cm/3–4 in beyond each end of the meat, and be about 15 cm/6 in across its width. Place a drip-tray (pan) directly under the spit-holder, and arrange the spit on it, with its motor attachment. The thickest part of the meat should be about 13 cm/5 in above the coals.

Since a long narrow roast will cook faster than a thick, stubby one, insert a meat thermometer in the fleshiest part of the meat, but not touching the bone or spit. Start up the motor, and cook, basting from time to time, until the meat thermometer registers 63–71°C/145–160°F. Maintain a constant temperature. Remove the meat when done, take it off the spit, and leave to rest on a board for about 15 minutes before carving it.

Serves 8–10.

OTHER LAMB RECIPES

Grilled Kofta (Minced Meat Kebabs)

INGREDIENTS	Metric	Imperial	American
Day-old bread slices	3	3	3
White wine	3 tbsp	3 tbsp	3 tbsp
Lamb from leg or shoulder, minced (ground)	450 g	1 lb	1 lb
Medium onion, chopped	1	1	1
Egg	1	1	1
Parsley sprigs, leaves only	4	4	4
Salt and black pepper			
Olive oil			

Cut the crusts off the bread and moisten it with the wine and a little water if needed. Squeeze it quite dry and put it with all the other ingredients except the olive oil in a food processor. Process until very smooth and pasty. With floured hands shape into rissoles the size of small egs, and leave to stand on a cake rack for 30 minutes, then mould the kofta round flattened 'shish kebab' skewers. Brush with olive oil. Make sure the fire is hot. Cook, turning often, until well browned on all sides. Serve on bread with Two-Way Yoghurt Dressing 1 (page 41).

Every Middle Eastern country has its own types of kofta; Turkey alone has dozens of different ones. This is a fairly basic version. You could make beef ones using butcher's mince if it is easier to get than minced lamb. In this case use soft breadcrumbs instead of the day-old bread and wine, and add a little extra flavouring such as a pinch of ground coriander or chilli powder.

Rosé Lamb Steaks

INGREDIENTS	Metric	Imperial	American
Lamb steaks cut from the leg, 2.5 cm/1 in thick	8	8	8
Marinade			
Salad oil	150 ml	¼ pt	½ cup + 2 tbsp
Lemon juice	150 ml	¼ pt	½ cup + 2 tbsp
Rosé wine	150 ml	¼ pt	½ cup + 2 tbsp
Garlic cloves, crushed	2	2	2
Rosemary sprigs	3–4	3–4	3–4
Salt and pepper			
Chopped parsley	2 tbsp	2 tbsp	2 tbsp

Place the steaks in a shallow dish. Mix together the marinade ingredients, and pour the mixture over the meat. Marinate for 2 hours.

Drain the meat over the marinade; keep it for basting. Place the meat on a lightly greased barbecue grill, 10–15 cm/4–6 in above medium heat, and cook for 20–25 minutes, turning and basting frequently.

Serves 8.

Devilled Lamb Chops

INGREDIENTS	Metric	Imperial	American
French mustard	2 tbsp	2 tbsp	2 tbsp
Soft brown sugar	225 g	8 oz	1¼ cups
Lamb chump (English) chops	8	8	8
Salt and pepper			

Mix together the mustard and sugar, adding a little extra mustard or a few drops of vinegar if needed to make a paste. Season the chops on both sides with salt and pepper, and spread one side of each chop with mustard-sugar mixture. Place a lightly greased grill 10–15 cm/4–6 in above the coals. Put the chops on the grill, coated side up, and grill over medium heat for 5–8 minutes. Turn over, spread with remaining mustard-sugar mixture and cook for a further 5–8 minutes.

Serves 8.

Sasaties
(Sweet Curried Skewered Lamb)

INGREDIENTS	Metric	Imperial	American
Fat leg of lamb	1.5 kg	3 lb	3 lb
Garlic clove	½	½	½
Large onions skinned	4	4	4
Light soft brown sugar	2 tbsp	2 tbsp	2 tbsp
Milk	275 ml	½ pt	1¼ cups
Lamb dripping	1 tbsp	1 tbsp	1 tbsp
Sweetened lime juice cordial (undiluted)	1 tbsp	1 tbsp	1 tbsp
Curry powder	1 tbsp	1 tbsp	1 tbsp
Whole cloves	½ tsp	½ tsp	½ tsp
Whole allspice	½ tsp	½ tsp	½ tsp
White wine vinegar	125 ml	4 fl oz	½ cup
Salt and pepper			
Melted lamb dripping for brushing			
Flour	1 tbsp	1 tbsp	1 tbsp
Chilled butter	1 tbsp	1 tbsp	1 tbsp

Cut the lamb into 5 cm/2 in cubes, fat and lean together. Rub the inside of a large earthenware bowl with the cut side of the garlic clove. Lay the meat in the bowl. Slice 2 onions, add them to the meat with the sugar, and pour the milk over them. Slice the remaining 2 onions, and fry them in the dripping until lightly browned. Add the lime juice, whole spices, vinegar and seasoning. Pour the whole lot over the meat and leave overnight.

Remove the meat and onions with a slotted spoon. Thread them on 6 skewers, alternating meat and onions. Pat dry, and brush with melted dripping.

Before cooking the sasaties, turn the marinade into a saucepan. Sprinkle the flour over it. Bring to the boil, stirring constantly, and cook until slightly thickened. Stir in the chilled butter.

Cook the sasaties on the barbecue grill, turning several times, for about 20 minutes or until cooked through. Serve with Yellow Rice (page 92), fruit chutney (sweet pickles) and a green salad, and with the sauce in a jug.

Apart from steaks, sasaties are one of the most popular foods at a South African *braaivleis* (pronounced bryflace) which is the local name for a barbecue. Actually a real braaivleis isn't quite like a barbecue as we know it. A fairly deep trench is dug in an open space, and a layer of dry wood and charcoal is put in the bottom and lit. When this is smouldering well, more fuel is added, and this is repeated until the trench is ½–⅔rd full. Sturdy wire grids are then laid over the centre part of the trench to grill the food on.

Only raw steaks and chops and perhaps boerewors (sausages) and sasaties are cooked as a rule, and only chunks of bread with butter, green salad and fresh fruit are served with them, but there is always plenty of beer. In fact South Africans are even known to douse the barbecue flare-ups with beer. They say it makes the smoke smell wonderful.

Chelow Kabab

INGREDIENTS	Metric	Imperial	American
Boneless mutton from leg or shoulder	750 g	1½ lb	1½ lb
Salt	1½ tsp	1½ tsp	1½ tsp
Pinch of pepper			
Natural yoghurt	175 ml	6 fl oz	¾ cup
Oil for cooking			
Tomatoes, halved	4	4	4
Potato crisps			
Optional			
Long-grain rice	350 g	12 oz	2 cups
Salt			
Egg yolks	4	4	4
Butter	50 g	2 oz	¼ cup

Cut the mutton into strips about 7 × 2 in/17.5 × 5 cm in size. Rub salt and pepper into both sides well. Marinate them in yoghurt for 3 hours. While marinating, season the tomatoes and brush with oil.

Weave the meat strips lengthways onto long skewers. Beat them out flat with a mallet. Oil them lightly. Cook them on a lightly greased grill 10–15 cm/4–6 in above medium heat, for 10–12 minutes. Meanwhile, cook the tomatoes in a double-sided grill over the coals. Put the crisps in a biscuit tin with holes punched in it, and heat through on the coals. Serve all three items together.

Traditionally these kababs are served with rice boiled in salted water. The rice is put in individual bowls with an egg yolk and dab of butter in the centre of each bowl. The egg and butter are mashed into the hot rice and eaten with the meat. Instead of crisps, you could cook the rice ahead and keep it hot in a food flask if you are making the kababs as the single main dish for a small group.

Note
If you cannot get mutton, use well-aged lamb.

Sweet and Spicy Noisettes

INGREDIENTS	Metric	Imperial	American
Clear honey	1 tbsp	1 tbsp	1 tbsp
Dry mustard	2 tsp	2 tsp	2 tsp
Salt and pepper			
Lemon juice	1 tbsp	1 tbsp	1 tbsp
Garlic clove, crushed	1	1	1
Lamb noisettes cut from loin	8	8	8
425 g/15 oz can of pineapple rings in natural juice	1 can (8 rings)	1 can (8 rings)	1 can (8 rings)
Butter or margarine	50 g	2 oz	¼ cup
Chopped fresh mint	4 tsp	4 tsp	4 tsp

Mix together the honey, mustard, seasoning, lemon juice and garlic. Spread the mixture over the noisettes and leave for 20 minutes.

Drain the juice from the pineapple. Put 4 tbsp juice and the fat into a small saucepan, and heat on the barbecue grill until the butter melts. Simmer for 5 minutes. Remove from the heat, and add the mint. Put the pan on the side of the grill to keep warm.

Brush the noisettes with this pineapple baste. Place on the lightly greased grill, 10–15 cm/4–6 in above medium heat, and cook for 30–35 minutes, turning and basting with pineapple mixture several times. 7–8 minutes before the end of the cooking time, place the pineapple rings on the grill to heat through. To serve, place 1 noisette on each pineapple ring and pour any remaining baste over the meat.

Serves 8.

Spicy Lamb Ribs

INGREDIENTS	Metric	Imperial	American
Large breasts of lamb	3–4	3–4	3–4
Marinade			
Cider	275 ml	½ pt	1¼ cups
Worcestershire sauce	4 tbsp	4 tbsp	4 tbsp
Demerara (brown crystal) sugar	50 g	2 oz	¼ cup
Red wine vinegar	4 tbsp	4 tbsp	4 tbsp
Finely chopped onion	50 g	2 oz	⅓ cup
Dried rosemary leaves	1 tsp	1 tsp	1 tsp
Salt and pepper			
Lemon	1	1	1

Cut through the meat between the bones with a sharp knife, and place in a shallow dish. Mix together the marinade ingredients in a saucepan, and bring to the boil. Simmer for 3–4 minutes. Cool.

Pour the cold marinade over the lamb ribs and leave for at least 3 hours, turning the meat occasionally. Drain the ribs over the marinade, and keep it for basting. Cook on a lightly greased grill 10–15 cm/4–6 in above medium heat for 12–16 minutes, turning and basting frequently. Cook until crisp and golden-brown. Serve with lemon wedges.

Serves 8–10.

Honey-Marinated Lamb or Pork Steaks

INGREDIENTS	Metric	Imperial	American
Tomato ketchup (catsup)	150 ml	$\frac{1}{4}$ pt	$\frac{1}{2}$ cup + 2 tbsp
Clear honey	2 tbsp	2 tbsp	2 tbsp
Lemon juice	2 tbsp	2 tbsp	2 tbsp
Corn oil	2 tbsp	2 tbsp	2 tbsp
Worcestershire sauce	1 tbsp	1 tbsp	1 tbsp
Lamb steaks cut from leg, or thick slices of pork	4	4	4
Tomatoes	4	4	4

Mix together the ketchup (catsup), honey, lemon juice, oil and Worcestershire sauce in a saucepan. Warm through on the stove indoors, stirring until blended. Pour the mixture over the steaks, placed in a shallow dish, and leave for at least 30 minutes, turning once. Drain the steaks over the marinade, and keep it for basting.

Cook the steaks on the lightly greased grill 10–15 cm/4–6 in above medium heat for about 8 minutes on each side, turning once and basting often with marinade. Add the tomatoes to the grill for the last 6–7 minutes of the cooking time.

PORK AND HAM

PORK AND HAM BASICS

Basic Recipe: Grilled Ham Steak

The dramatic way to present ham is to have a steak cut right across the thickest centre part of a whole ham. But smaller, individual steaks, often available vacuum-packed, are equally tasty. Make sure they are thick enough, and brush them with a spicy glaze while cooking.

INGREDIENTS	Metric	Imperial	American
Centre cut ham slice, weight about			
800 g/1¾ lb, cut 2.5 cm/1 in thick	*1*	*1*	*1*
OR	**OR**	**OR**	**OR**
Individual steaks of the same			
thickness	*4–5*	*4–5*	*4–5*
Easy ham glaze			
Clear honey	*3 tbsp*	*3 tbsp*	*3 tbsp*
Worcestershire sauce	*1 tbsp*	*1 tbsp*	*1 tbsp*
Dry mustard	*1 tbsp*	*1 tbsp*	*1 tbsp*
Ground ginger	*¾ tsp*	*¾ tsp*	*¾ tsp*
Ground black pepper			

Trim excess fat off the steak(s) and nick the edges at equal intervals. Mix the glaze ingredients well, making sure that the dry ingredients are blended in.

Place the ham on a lightly greased grill 10–15 cm/4–6 in above the coals. Cook, turning and basting with glaze, for 15–20 minutes or until browned and thoroughly heated.

Basic Recipe: Grilled Pork Chops

Pork chops grilled slowly and thoroughly lend themselves to many sweet-sour and fruity marinades and bastes. They are especially good cooked in a covered grill, and given a smoky flavour by adding hickory chips to the coals.

INGREDIENTS | Metric | Imperial | American
Loin pork chops 2.5 cm/1 in thick | 4 | 4 | 4
Salt and pepper

Trim any rind and excess fat off the chops before grilling. Place the chops on a lightly greased grill 10–15 cm/4–6 in above the coals. Grill slowly, turning once, for 15–20 minutes on each side or until the meat near the bone is no longer pink when exposed. Season with salt and pepper to taste.

Basic Recipe: Sausages and Hot Dogs

A barbecued hot dog in a roll becomes an exciting novelty when you substitute a choice of assorted sausages, breads and condiments for the usual ingredients. For instance, you might choose smoked sausages, garlic-flavoured knackwurst, turkey sausages, or pieces of a slim boiling sausage. If you choose these or other sausages which need precooking such as Spanish chorizo, simmer them for about 20 minutes, then drain them well before grilling. Allow 125–225 g/¼–½ lb of frankfurters or other sausages per person.

Interesting breads instead of the usual long rolls can also give your hot dogs a new character. Poppy seed rolls, whole-wheat snack rolls, or pitta bread make delicious wrappers for grilled sausages and frankfurters. Serve them filled with a generous choice of condiments inside – or pile these on split rolls as open sandwiches.

Variously-flavoured mustards are easy to buy and popular, but offer some of the following too: tomato or mushroom ketchup (catsup), chilli sauce, horseradish cream, sliced onions and tomatoes, piccalilli and other pickles and relished such as pickled beetroot and gherkins.

INGREDIENTS | Metric | Imperial | American
Frankfurters or other sausages | | |
* weighing about 50 g/2 oz each* | 900 g | 2 lb | 2 lb
Long hot dog rolls (buns) or other | | |
* bread 'carriers'* | 16–20 | 16–20 | 16–20

Place the frankfurters or other sausages, boiled and drained if required, on a lightly greased grill 10–15 cm/4–6 in above the coals. Cook, turning often, until done as you like them, and well heated through. Place split rolls, cut side down, around the edge of the barbecue, to toast if you wish. Serve with the condiments above in small bowls, with spoons for serving.

Basic Recipe: Oven-Barbecued Spareribs

Spareribs take up so much space on the grill for an hour or more that many people oven-cook them first, then just reheat and crisp them on the barbecue in small batches. It's a particularly good method if you are trying to serve a large number of people, because you can have freshly heated batches ready whenever people want to eat them.

Make sure you get meaty American cut spareribs from the lower fore loin, sometimes sold in England as pork rib bones. You should be able to buy them in large slabs or cut into serving portions of 2–3 ribs each. If you oven-cook them in slabs, turn them over half-way through cooking, and divide them before putting them on the barbecue.

If you will marinate the ribs as well as basting them, prepare the marinade ahead; see the choice on pages 23–4. Make sure you prepare enough for basting as well. Pour the marinade over the ribs, and leave for at least 4 hours, preferably overnight.

INGREDIENTS	Metric	Imperial	American
Marinade, optional (page 23)			
Lean pork spareribs cut in serving portions	*1.6–1.8 kg*	*3½–4 lb*	*3½–4 lb*
Baste, if not using marinade (page 23–4)			

If you marinate the ribs, drain them over the marinade and keep it for basting. Arrange the ribs, fat side up, in a shallow roasting tin (pan). Cook, uncovered, at 180°C/350°F/Gas Mark 4 for 1¼ hours, basting with marinade or a baste occasionally. Drain off excess fat.

When ready to barbecue, place the ribs on a lightly greased grill, 10–15 cm/4–6 in above the coals. Cook, basting with marinade or baste, and turning the ribs often, for 15–20 minutes or until crisp and well browned all over.

OTHER PORK AND HAM RECIPES

Bacon Chops in Ale

INGREDIENTS	Metric	Imperial	American
Bacon chops (unsmoked)	6	6	6
Beer	275 ml	½ pt	1¼ cups
Freshly ground black pepper			
Bay leaf	1	1	1
Onions, sliced	3	3	3
Black treacle (molasses)	60 ml	2 fl oz	¼ cup
Juice of ½ lemon			
Oil for frying			

Put the bacon chops in a shallow dish. Add the beer, pepper, bay leaf and sliced onion. Cover and refrigerate overnight. Strain off the beer marinade into a saucepan. Start the bacon chops cooking on the barbecue (or under the grill). Boil the beer marinade until reduced by half, then add the treacle (molasses) and lemon juice. Brush the marinade over the chops as a baste, turn them and rebaste. Continue cooking until tender and glazed for 13–18 minutes in all. Put the remaining onions in a stout frying pan, sprinkle with oil and fry on the barbecue grill until soft. Cover the chops with them and with any remaining marinade.

Honey-Basted Pork Chops

INGREDIENTS	Metric	Imperial	American
Large pork chops	6	6	6
Ground black pepper			
Clear honey, warmed	3 tbsp	3 tbsp	3 tbsp
Dry cider	225 ml	8 fl oz	1 cup
Powdered sage	2 tsp	2 tsp	2 tsp

Season the chops well with pepper. Put them in a shallow dish. Mix the honey, cider and sage together and pour over the chops. Leave to marinate for 1 hour, turning once. Cook on barbecue, turning as needed and basting often with the cider-honey mixture, for about 13 minutes on each side or until cooked through and well glazed. Serve with any remaining baste as a sauce if you wish.

Spicy Ham Steak

A fruity baste flavoured with clove and pineapple impregnates this fine, juicy steak. Equally good barbecued at home, or carried in its marinade to a picnic spot.

INGREDIENTS	Metric	Imperial	American
Melted butter or margarine	50 g	2 oz	$\frac{1}{4}$ cup
Dry sherry	225 ml	8 fl oz	1 cup
Pineapple juice from carton	225 ml	8 fl oz	1 cup
Ground cloves	2 tsp	2 tsp	2 tsp
Mild paprika pepper	2 tsp	2 tsp	2 tsp
Dry mustard	$\frac{1}{4}$ tsp	$\frac{1}{4}$ tsp	$\frac{1}{4}$ tsp
Firmly packed soft brown sugar	$\frac{1}{4}$ tsp	$\frac{1}{4}$ tsp	$\frac{1}{4}$ tsp
Garlic clove, finely chopped or squeezed (minced or pressed)	1	1	1
Ham slice 2.5 cm/1 in thick cut right through thickest part of a whole ham	1	1	1
OR	**OR**	**OR**	**OR**
Individual steaks of the same thickness	4–5	4–5	4–5

Mix together thoroughly all the ingredients except the ham. Pour the marinade/baste over the ham in a shallow dish, cover and refrigerate for at least 3 hours.

Drain the ham slice(s) over the marinade and keep it for basting. Place the slice(s) on a lightly greased grill 10–15 cm/4–6 in above medium-hot coals. Cook, turning and basting often, for about 20 minutes or until browned and well heated through.

Sherry-Flavoured Ham

A large, fully cooked bone-in ham will serve about 25 people. If you wish, add soaked hickory wood chips to the coals for the last hour of cooking, to give the ham an old-style smoky flavour.

INGREDIENTS	Metric	Imperial	American
5.4–6.3 kg/12–14 lb ham, fully cooked	1	1	1
Prepared mustard	3 tbsp	3 tbsp	3 tbsp
Ground cloves	2 tsp	2 tsp	2 tsp
Dry sherry or orange juice	225 ml	8 fl oz	1 cup

With a sharp knife, score the top of the ham in a criss-cross pattern, cutting about 6 mm/¼ in deep. Rub the surface with mustard, and sprinkle with cloves.

Bank the fire on each side of the fire-bowl, and place a metal drip-tray (pan) in the centre. Place the grill 10–15 cm/4–6 in above the coals. Insert a meat thermometer into the thickest part of the meat, without letting it touch the bone.

Place the ham on the grill, directly over the drip-tray. Cover the barbecue, and adjust the dampers according to the manufacturer's directions. Cook for about 2½ hours, maintaining a constant temperature.

After 2 hours, soak hickory chips in water for 30 minutes. Drain them, and add them to the coals. Begin basting the ham with sherry or orange juice every 15 minutes. Continue cooking until the meat thermometer registers 60°C/140°F; this takes 3–3½ hours.

Cidered Sausage Skuets

INGREDIENTS	Metric	Imperial	American
Cider baste			
Medium dry cider	6 tbsp	6 tbsp	6 tbsp
Clear honey	6 tbsp	6 tbsp	6 tbsp
Tomato paste	3 tbsp	3 tbsp	3 tbsp
Juice of 1 lemon			
Skuets			
Large English pork sausages (50g/2 oz each)	1.5 kg	3 lb	3 lb
Thin streaky bacon rashers without rind (strips)	12	12	12
Small button mushrooms	225 g	8 oz	½ lb
Oil			
Salt and pepper			

Shortly ahead of time, stir the baste ingredients in a saucepan over medium heat until well blended.

Pinch the sausages in the middle, then twist them to make 2 short links of each. Separate the links. Wrap each in a bacon rasher. Thread the stubby sausages onto 12 kebab skewers alternately with the button mushrooms. Brush with oil and season lightly. Cook on the barbecue, turning often and brushing with the baste, until cooked through. If serving on plates, spoon a little extra baste over each skuet before serving.

Sweet and Sour Pork Chops

Pork chops, carrots and apple rings all cook together fast in this festive barbecue dinner. The sweet-sour baste which glazes the meat is also used for the sauce spooned over individual portions when serving.

INGREDIENTS	Metric	Imperial	American
Light soft brown sugar	75 g	3 oz	3 oz
Red wine vinegar	125 ml	4 fl oz	$\frac{1}{2}$ cup
Soy sauce	2 tsp	2 tsp	2 tsp
Dry sherry	2 tsp	2 tsp	2 tsp
Tomato ketchup (catsup)	50 ml	2 fl oz	$\frac{1}{4}$ cup
Sweet-sour sauce (see below)			
Loin pork chops cut 2.5 cm/1 in thick	4	4	4
Small, whole cooked carrots	8–12	8–12	8–12
Large eating apples, unpeeled, cored and cut into 2 cm/$\frac{3}{4}$ in rounds	4	4	4

Sweet-sour sauce			
Chicken stock	150 ml	$\frac{1}{4}$ pt	$\frac{2}{3}$ cup
Cornflour (cornstarch)	1 tbsp	1 tbsp	1 tbsp
Corn oil	1 tbsp	1 tbsp	1 tbsp
Garlic clove	1	1	1
Large onion, thinly sliced	1	1	1

Mix together the sugar, vinegar, soy sauce, sherry and ketchup (catsup). Keep aside 125 ml/4 fl oz $\frac{1}{2}$ cup of this baste for the sauce. Use the rest to baste the meat while cooking.

Trim the chops, and nick the edges. Place the chops on a lightly greased grill, 10–15 cm/4–6 in above medium-hot coals. Cook, turning and basting often, for about 10 minutes. Add the carrots and apple slices. Continue cooking, turning and basting them all, until the meat is fully cooked through and the carrots and apple slices are hot and well browned (about 10 minutes longer).

While they are cooking, make the sauce. Stir a little stock into the cornflour to make it creamy, then blend in the rest with the reserved baste. Warm the corn oil in a frying pan over medium-high heat. Squeeze (press) in the garlic and onion. Cook, stirring constantly, until the onion is soft. Stir in the cornflour mixture and stir until thickened.

Serve the chops with the sauce spooned over them.

Skewered Pork Meatballs with Apples

An unusual and beguiling barbecue treat of fresh minced (ground) pork balls and apple quarters with bacon strips woven between them in rippling patterns.

INGREDIENTS

	Metric	Imperial	American
Minced (ground) lean fresh pork	700 g	$1\frac{1}{2}$ lb	$1\frac{1}{2}$ lb
Egg, beaten	1	1	1
Fine dry white breadcrumbs	25 g	1 oz	$\frac{1}{3}$ cup
Finely chopped onion	50 g	2 oz	$\frac{1}{3}$ cup
Apple juice	2 tbsp	2 tbsp	2 tbsp
Salt	$\frac{1}{2}$ tsp	$\frac{1}{2}$ tsp	$\frac{1}{2}$ tsp
Ground ginger	$\frac{1}{2}$ tsp	$\frac{1}{2}$ tsp	$\frac{1}{2}$ tsp
Powdered dry sage	$\frac{1}{4}$ tsp	$\frac{1}{4}$ tsp	$\frac{1}{4}$ tsp
Pepper	$\frac{1}{4}$ tsp	$\frac{1}{4}$ tsp	$\frac{1}{4}$ tsp
Large Golden Delicious apples, cored and quartered	2	2	2
Long back rashers (strips) of bacon with rind removed	8	8	8

You will need 4 long kebab skewers for this dish.

Make the meatballs first. Mix together thoroughly the pork, beaten egg, breadcrumbs, onion, apple juice, salt, ginger, sage and pepper. Divide the mixture into 16 equal portions, and shape each into a ball. Leave for 15 minutes to firm up.

To assemble the skewers, pierce one end of a bacon rasher (strip) with a skewer, then push on a pork ball. Pierce the bacon again, leaving a little space between it and the meatball, and add an apple quarter to the skewer. Pierce the bacon as before, push on another meatball, and then pierce the bacon end. The bacon should form equal S-curves around the meat and apple. Repeat, so that the skewer has two bacon rashers (strips), 4 pork meatballs and 2 apple quarters, all spaced fairly loosely so that the bacon will brown evenly. Fill the remaining skewers in the same way.

Place the skewers on a lightly greased grill 10–15 cm/4–6 in above medium-hot coals. Cook, turning gently as needed to brown evenly, for 15–20 minutes, until bacon is crisp and pork is no longer pink inside.

POULTRY

POULTRY BASICS

Basic Recipe: Spit-Roasted Chicken and Other Birds

Your tender chicken, turkey, duck or any other bird will be golden and succulent if spit-roasted because the turning spit cooks it evenly. It also makes it partly self-basting because any baste not absorbed rolls over the bird's skin instead of dripping off immediately.

INGREDIENTS	Metric	Imperial	American
Whole oven-ready roasting chicken, 1.4–1.6 kg/3–3½ lb, thawed if frozen	1	1	1
Marinade or baste, optional (pages 24–5)			
Salt			

Choose a chicken 10–11.5 cm/4–4½ in wide. Remove the giblets for another use, then rinse the bird and pat dry. Marinate it if you wish for 2–8 hours depending on the mixture you choose.

Drain the bird if marinated, reserving the marinade for basting. Truss the wings and legs securely against the body in as even a shape as possible. Run the barbecue spit through the bird from vent end to neck end, exactly in the centre so that the weight is evenly distributed. Fix with spit forks. Pick up the spit at both ends and turn it. If one side tends to pull downward, re-position the spit a little more towards that side or add a balance weight on the lighter side. When the bird is evenly balanced, secure the spit forks so that they will not loosen during cooking.

Arrange a bed of hot coals parallel with the spit and extending 7.5–10 cm/3–4 in beyond each end of the chicken. It should be about 15 cm/6 in wide, with the front edge sited about 5 cm/2 in clear of the spit. Place a metal drip-tray (pan) directly under and in front of the spit. The surface of the bird should be about 13 cm/5 in above the coals.

Position the spit on the barbecue, and start the motor. As the bird cooks, maintain an even temperature.

The cooking time for the size and type of bird suggested above is 80–90 minutes or until a meat thermometer inserted into the fleshiest part of the thigh (but not touching the bone or spit) registers 82–85°C/180–185°F. When the bird begins to turn a good brown colour, test to see if it is done. Protect your hands with soft paper, and press the thick part of a thigh; if it is soft, the bird is ready.

When the bird is ready, push or rake the coals away, and let the bird turn on the spit without heat for 3–5 minutes before carving. Sprinkle it with a little salt as it turns.

Turkey
Follow the instructions for spit-roasting a chicken with these differences: choose a bird weighing 5.4–6.3 kg/12–14 lb, and 19–20 cm/$7\frac{1}{2}$–8 in wide. Cook for $4\frac{1}{4}$–$4\frac{1}{2}$ hours or until a meat thermometer inserted into the thigh registers 82–85°C/180–185°F.

Guineafowl
Spit-roast like chicken for 70–90 minutes.

Domestic duck
Spit-roast like chicken except as follows: choose a bird weighing 1.8–2.3 kg/4–5 lb and 11.5–12.5 cm/$4\frac{1}{2}$–5 in wide. While it cooks, prick the skin to release the fat under it. Cook for $1\frac{1}{4}$–$1\frac{3}{4}$ hours.

Basic Recipe: Chicken on a Covered Grill

Here is a foolproof method of barbecuing a whole chicken. Since its cover converts a barbecue into an oven, the bird cooks slowly and evenly until golden-brown all over.

INGREDIENTS	Metric	Imperial	American
Whole oven-ready roasting chicken, 1.4 – 1.6 kg/ 3–3½ lb, thawed if frozen	*1*	*1*	*1*
Marinade or baste, optional (pages 24–5)			
Salt			

Remove the giblets for other uses, then rinse the bird and pat dry. Truss or re-truss if required. Marinate for 2–8 hours if you wish or stuff the bird with your preferred stuffing. (Only salt the bird *after* cooking.)

Bank the fire equally on each side of the fire-bowl, and place a metal drip-tray (pan) in the centre. Place the grill 10–15 cm/4–6 in above the drip-tray. Grease the grill lightly.

Drain the bird if marinated, and reserve the marinade for basting. Insert a meat thermometer into the fleshy part of a thigh but not touching the bone. Place the chicken breast side up on the grill directly over the drip-tray. Cover the barbecue and adjust the dampers according to the manufacturer's directions.

Cook for about 30 minutes, then baste. Continue cooking, basting every 10 minutes, until chicken is cooked (about 60 minutes in all or when meat thermometer registers 82–85°C/180–185°F – allow 10–15 minutes extra if stuffed). The bird's joints should move easily in the sockets, and the juices should run clear when the skin is pierced.

Basic Recipe: Chicken Portions

If you barbecue on an open grill, the best way to cook chicken is in serving portions, quarters or halves. They lie fairly flat, so cook by direct heat from the coals. It is cheaper to cut up a bird or birds yourself than to buy ready-cut portions.

INGREDIENTS	Metric	Imperial	American
Whole oven-ready roasting chicken, 1.4 – 1.6 kg/ 3–3½ lb, cut into portions, quarters or halves	1	1	1
Marinade or baste, optional (pages 24–5)			
Salt			

Rinse the chicken pieces and pat dry. For quarters and halves, hook the wing-tips back behind the body-limb joint. Marinate the pieces if you wish, for 1–2 hours. (Only salt the meat *after* cooking, to keep it moist and juicy.)

Brush the chicken pieces with a baste, or, if marinated, drain, reserving the marinade. Arrange the chicken pieces, skin side up, on a lightly greased grill, 10–15 cm/4–6 in above medium-hot coals.

Cook, turning and basting occasionally with either baste or reserved marinade, for the following times:

40–50 minutes for leg portions, quarters or halves;

about 30 minutes for breast pieces, thighs or large drumsticks;

about 20 minutes for small drumsticks or wings.

The chicken is ready when the meat near the bone is no longer pink when cut open.

OTHER POULTRY RECIPES

Honeyed Chicken Drumsticks

INGREDIENTS	Metric	Imperial	American
Chicken drumsticks	10	10	10
Clear honey	4 tbsp	4 tbsp	4 tbsp
Juice of 1 lemon			
Salt and pepper			
Demerara sugar (golden crystal)	6 tbsp	6 tbsp	6 tbsp

Prick the chicken all over with a skewer. Heat the honey and lemon juice together and brush it over the drumsticks. Season with salt and pepper, then roll each drumstick in demerara sugar. Cook on the barbecue, turning often, for 20 minutes or until golden and tender. The sugar will make a crunchy coating. Wrap a foil around the bone end of each drumstick for easy eating. Serve with Bacon-Wrapped Corn (page 94) and foil-wrapped jacket potatoes filled with soured cream.

Pekin Duck

True Chinese Pekin Duck consists of 5 cm/2 in pieces of crisp duck skin and the fat underneath it also carefully crisped, wrapped in warmed, soft thin flour-and-water pancakes. The duck meat is only eaten afterwards. However, no hungry barbecuer wants to wait for cooled duck meat, so in this recipe, the skin and meat are served together.

INGREDIENTS	Metric	Imperial	American
Ducklings, weighing 1.8–2 kg/4–4½ lb, thawed if frozen	2	2	2
Ground ginger	1 tsp	1 tsp	1 tsp
Ground cinnamon	1 tsp	1 tsp	1 tsp
Grated nutmeg	½ tsp	½ tsp	½ tsp
Ground cloves	¼ tsp	¼ tsp	¼ tsp
Pepper	¼ tsp	¼ tsp	¼ tsp
Soy sauce	50 ml	2 fl oz	¼ cup
Hoi Sin Sauce (see note)	225 ml	8 fl oz	1 cup
Pancakes (crêpes) about 12.5 cm/5 in across, made ahead	12–18	12–18	12–18
Spring onions (scallions) including a few tops, finely sliced	18	18	18
Fresh coriander leaves, chopped (see note)	40 g	1½ oz	½ cup

Remove the birds' giblets, and keep for another use. Prick the skins of the ducklings well with a fork. Trim off any excess neck skin, fold over the flap of remaining skin and secure to the back with a poultry skewer.

Mix together the ginger, cinnamon, nutmeg, cloves and pepper. Dust about ½ tsp of this spice mixture inside each duck, then rub the remaining mixture over the outsides of the birds. Leave the body cavities open to aid even cooking.

Bank a hot fire equally on each side of the fire-bowl, and place a deep metal drip-pan in the centre. Put the birds, breast up, on a lightly greased grill 10–15 cm/4–6 in above the drip-pan. Cover the barbecue, leaving the dampers open to maintain a hot fire at a constant temperature.

Mix together the soy sauce and 2 tbsp of the Hoi Sin Sauce. Put the remaining Hoi Sin Sauce, and the sliced onion (scallion) and chopped coriander in 3 separate serving bowls, ready for use.

Arrange the pancakes in stacks of six, and cut each stack in half (easier to do than halving the pancakes singly). Wrap each pile of halves in foil, and place on the edge of the grill for the last ½ hour of the cooking time, to warm through.

Cook the ducklings for 2–2¼ hours, or until the thigh meat is soft when squeezed (protect your hands with soft paper when squeezing). For the last 20 minutes of the cooking time, baste the ducklings often with the soy mixture.

To serve, spread warm pancake halves with Hoi Sin Sauce. Slice small pieces of crisp duck skin and flesh (trimming out fat) and lay on each pancake half; add some onion and coriander, and wrap the pancake around them all. Eat as finger food.

Serves 8.

Notes
1. Hoi Sin Sauce is a thick soy sauce made commercially. Ask for it at any store which sells oriental foods.
2. If you cannot get fresh coriander leaves, use celery leaves.

Marinated Chicken

INGREDIENTS	Metric	Imperial	American
Marinade			
Lemon juice	2 tbsp	2 tbsp	2 tbsp
Oil	3 tbsp	3 tbsp	3 tbsp
Worcestershire sauce	1 tbsp	1 tbsp	1 tbsp
Garlic clove, crushed	1	1	1
Tomato ketchup (catsup)	2 tbsp	2 tbsp	2 tbsp
Freshly ground black pepper			
Tabasco to taste			
Chicken			
Chicken quarters	4	4	4
Seasoned flour			
Oil	2 tbsp	2 tbsp	2 tbsp

Mix together all the marinade ingredients. Put in a large plastic bag. Prick the chicken quarters all over with a knife point, and add them to the bag. Close it securely, and refrigerate for several hours or overnight, turning 2 or 3 times.

Take the chicken out of the marinade, and roll in seasoned flour. Sprinkle with oil. Cook on the barbecue, turning often for 40 minutes or until golden and tender. Brush with marinade during cooking if you wish.

Jacket potatoes, topped with cheese and a small piece of preserved ginger, are a delicious addition to this spicy way of serving chicken.

Chicken Brochettes with Prunes

INGREDIENTS	Metric	Imperial	American
Stuffed olives	24	24	24
Prunes, soaked, cooked and stoned	24	24	24
Chicken drumsticks, boned	16	16	16
Flour	2 tbsp	2 tbsp	2 tbsp
Ground ginger	½ tsp	½ tsp	½ tsp
Butter or margarine	50 g	2 oz	¼ cup
Oranges	4	4	4
Lemon Barbecue Baste			
Clear honey	4 tbsp	4 tbsp	4 tbsp
Lemon juice	7 tsp	7 tsp	7 tsp
Soy sauce	1 tbsp	1 tbsp	1 tbsp
A few grains of chilli powder			

Put a stuffed olive in the stone hollow in each prune, and press the prune to re-shape, enclosing the olive. Cut each drumstick in half across. Toss together the flour and ginger in a plastic bag. Add the chicken pieces, and toss until well coated. Melt the butter or margarine in a frying pan, add the chicken, and sauté, turning often, for 8–10 minutes. Cool slightly.

To make the baste, place all the baste ingredients in a saucepan and warm, stirring, until liquid.

Peel the oranges and cut each into 4 quarters lengthways, then cut each quarter in half across. Arrange 4 pieces of chicken, 3 pieces of orange and 3 prunes on each of 8 long skewers. Brush with the baste, and place on the barbecue grill placed 10–15 cm/4–6 in above the coals. Cook the brochettes, turning often and basting, for 15–25 minutes.

Serves 8.

Lemon and Rosemary Chicken

INGREDIENTS	Metric	Imperial	American
Chicken portions	4	4	4
Sprigs of rosemary			
Baste			
Butter or margarine	75 g	3 oz	3 oz
Lemon juice	2 tbsp	2 tbsp	2 tbsp
Salt	1 tsp	1 tsp	1 tsp
White pepper	¼ tsp	¼ tsp	¼ tsp
Paprika	¼ tsp	¼ tsp	¼ tsp

Wash the chicken portions and pat dry with soft kitchen paper. Melt the butter and mix with the other baste ingredients.

Lightly grease the barbecue grill, and place it 10–15 cm/4–6 in above medium-hot coals. Place the chicken portions on the grill; cook for 40 minutes, brushing with basting sauce occasionally, and turning every few minutes to ensure that the portions are cooked evenly. Just before the end of the cooking time, throw a few extra sprigs of rosemary on the coals to give a delicious scent and flavour to the chicken. Serve with grilled tomatoes.

Chicken Satay

INGREDIENTS	Metric	Imperial	American
Marinade			
Salt	1½ tsp	1½ tsp	1½ tsp
Freshly ground black			
pepper to taste			
Thick coconut milk			
(see below)	125 ml	4 fl oz	½ cup
Meat			
Medium (1.5 kg/3 lb.)			
chicken thawed if frozen	1	1	1
Sauce			
Smooth peanut butter	4 tbsp	4 tbsp	4 tbsp
Chilli powder	½ tsp	½ tsp	½ tsp
Lemon rind, grated	1 tsp	1 tsp	1 tsp
Soft brown sugar	1½ tsp	1½ tsp	1½ tsp
Water	225 ml	8 fl oz	1 cup
Juice of ½ lime			

Mix the seasonings and coconut milk. Skin the chicken, cut the meat off the bones and cut it into 3 cm/1½ in pieces. Marinate the pieces in the coconut milk mixture for 1–2 hours. Drain, reserving the marinade. Thread 4 pieces of meat tightly on 6 short skewers. Put aside.

To make the sauce, mix all the ingredients except the lime juice in a saucepan. Simmer for 20 minutes. Take off the heat and stir in the juice. Put in a vacuum flask.

Cook the chicken on the barbecue, turning as needed, for 12–18 minutes or until tender. Baste with marinade often while cooking. Serve with the satay sauce.

To make a fair substitute for coconut milk (obtained by grinding fresh coconut and squeezing it through a cloth), process 4 tbsp desiccated coconut in a blender adding 175 ml/6 fl oz/¾ cup hot water gradually, or use coconut cream sold in blocks at health food stores.

SEAFOOD

SEAFOOD BASICS

Basic Recipe: Fish Steaks and Fillets

All fish steaks and fillets need frequent basting while being bar-becued, to prevent them drying out. If you want to cook them directly on the grill, they must be at least 2 cm/¾ in thick. For thinner pieces, use a hinged fish broiler to prevent them breaking when being turned.

INGREDIENTS	Metric	Imperial	American
Fish steaks or fillets, weighing about 225 g/8 oz each, and cut 2.5 cm/ 1 in thick	6	6	6
Marinade or baste (pages 26–7)			

Wipe the fish with a damp cloth. If you marinate it, put the fish in a large plastic bag in a shallow non-metal dish, and pour in the marinade. Close the bag securely, refrigerate and marinate for 1–2 hours.

Drain the fish over the marinade, and keep it for basting. Arrange the fish pieces on a well-greased grill 10–15 cm/4–6 in above medium-hot coals. Cook, turning once and basting often with the marinade (or another baste if the fish is not marinated) for 15–20 minutes or until the thickest part of the fish flakes easily when pierced with a thin skewer.

Serves 6.

Basic Recipe: Large Whole Fish

Large whole fish – salmon, bass or any large fresh-water fish – are delicious when barbecued, but because of their size and weight, they need special handling. This recipe can be used for any fish weighing between 1.4 and 3.6 kg/3 and 8 lb. To calculate the number of helpings, allow 225 g/8 oz fish per person.

INGREDIENTS	Metric	Imperial	American
Whole fish (1.4–3.6 kg/3–8 lb)			
cleaned, scaled and with head			
removed if you wish	1	1	1
Salt and pepper			
Lemon, sliced	1	1	1
Onion, sliced	1	1	1
Parsley sprigs			

Wipe the fish with a damp cloth inside and out. Sprinkle the inside of the cavity with salt and pepper. Tuck inside it the lemon and onion slices, and several parsley sprigs. Cut a piece of doubled heavy-duty foil which fits exactly over one side of the fish when moulded to its shape smoothly. This is to give it protection and support. Press the folded foil smoothly against one side of the fish including the head and tail. Turn the fish and foil over, and insert a meat thermometer into the thickest part of the flesh if you wish; it must not touch the dorsal fin.

Bank the fire equally on both sides of the fire-bowl, and place the grill 10–15 cm/4–6 in above the coals. Place the fish, foil side down, over the space between the coals. Put a small wad of foil under the tail to hold it up, and to protect it slightly from the heat; being thin, it will cook faster than the rest of the flesh.

Cover the barbecue if using a covered grill, and adjust the dampers according to the manufacturer's directions. If you are cooking on an open grill, cut off enough wide heavy-duty foil to cover the grill *completely*; tuck it over the edges of the barbecue to seal in all the heat.

Allow 10 minutes cooking time per 2.5 cm/1 in thickness of fish, measured at the thickest part; for instance, a fish 7.5 cm/3 in thick will cook in 30 minutes. At the end of the calculated time, lift the cover or foil, and test whether the fish is ready. A meat thermometer should register 54–55°C/130°F and you should be able to run a thin skewer through the skin and flesh to the bone without resistance.

When the fish is ready, hold a warmed, flat serving platter close to the grill. Slide a wide metal spatula carefully under the foil beneath the fish, and lift off the fish and foil together. Ease the fish and foil onto the platter. Lift or scrape off the top layer of skin if you wish. Cut right down to the backbone of the fish with a serving knife. Then slide a spatula between the flesh and ribs, and lift off one helping at a time. When the top half of the fish has been served, lift off the backbone, cutting it free from the head if required. Then serve the lower half of the fish, taking care not to pick up any bits of foil with it.

OTHER SEAFOOD RECIPES

Grilled Sardines

INGREDIENTS	Metric	Imperial	American
Fresh sardines	12	12	12
Corn oil	2 tbsp	2 tbsp	2 tbsp
Herb Butter			
Fresh herbs, finely chopped (choose from parsley, chervil, chives, tarragon etc.)	6 tbsp	6 tbsp	6 tbsp
Softened butter	125 g	4 oz	½ cup
Garlic clove	1 small	1 small	1 small
Few drops of lemon juice			
Salt and pepper			

Ratatouille (page 93)

Clean the fish and brush them with the oil. Season to taste. Place in a fish broiler, and lay on a well-greased grill placed 10–15 cm/4–6 in over hot coals. Grill, turning once, for 10 minutes. Serve 3 fish to each person with pats of herb butter and with Ratatouille.

To make the *Herb Butter*, mix the herbs into the softened butter. Squeeze (press) in the garlic clove. Add the lemon juice, and blend in with a little seasoning. Chill until firm enough to mould. Shape into a roll, wrap in greaseproof (waxed) paper, and chill again. Slice into pats when needed.

Florida Fish Fillets

INGREDIENTS	Metric	Imperial	American
White fish fillets, skinned (cod, haddock, mullet, etc) 100–150 g/ 4–5 oz each			
For each fillet			
Butter for greasing			
Salt	1 tsp	1 tsp	1 tsp
Finely grated orange rind	1 tsp	1 tsp	1 tsp
Finely grated grapefruit rind	½ tsp	½ tsp	½ tsp
A few grains grated nutmeg			

Grease squares of foil big enough to enclose the fillets. Lay a fillet in the centre of each square. Sprinkle it with salt and rind. Fold the foil over the fish, allowing a good overlap. Fold over the ends in the same way. Cook the fish on the grill over hot coals for 25–30 minutes. Put the fish parcel on a plate, then open the foil and eat with a fork.

Spicy Skewered Prawns (Shrimp)

INGREDIENTS	Metric	Imperial	American
Large prawns (shrimp), shelled	450 g	1 lb	1 lb
Lemon wedges			
Marinade			
Chilli powder	1 tsp	1 tsp	1 tsp
White wine vinegar	1 tbsp	1 tbsp	1 tbsp
Garlic clove, crushed	1	1	1
Salt and black pepper			
Chopped parsley	1 tsp	1 tsp	1 tsp
Salad oil	6 tbsp	6 tbsp	6 tbsp

Make the marinade first. Mix all the ingredients, beating to blend them well. Place the shellfish in a plastic bag in a non-metallic bowl, and pour the marinade over them. Close the bag securely and marinate the prawns (shrimp) for 2 hours. Remove the prawns (shrimp) from the marinade, and drain. Thread onto 4 thin skewers. Keep the marinade for basting.

Place the skewers on a well-greased grill, 10–15 cm/4–6 in above medium-hot coals. Grill for 6–10 minutes, turning from time to time and basting with marinade.

Serve with lemon wedges for squeezing.

Butterflied Trout with Almond Butter

Trout can be marinated in a lemony French dressing before being barbecued-grilled.

INGREDIENTS	Metric	Imperial	American
Small trout, about 275 g/10 oz each, cleaned but with heads and tails left on	4	4	4
French Dressing made with 4 parts oil to 1 part each white wine vinegar and lemon juice (see page 39)	350 ml	12 fl oz	1½ cups
Butter or margarine	4 tbsp	4 tbsp	4 tbsp
Salted almonds, chopped small	75 g	3 oz	½ cup

Bone the trout first, leaving the heads and tails on. Cut off the fins, and split the fish along the belly from the body cavity to the tail. Hold the body cavity open, and insert a sharp pointed knife at the head end just beside the backbone where the ribs start; the sharp blade edge should be facing the tail. Ease the knife-point under the top ribs, and cut between the ribs and flesh all down that side, freeing the thin rib bones. Repeat on the second side. Now ease the backbone free, taking care to leave the back flesh of the trout intact. With kitchen scissors, snip through the backbone at the head and tail ends, and lift it out. Discard it. The fish should now be easy to 'butterfly', that is, to spread out flat.

Prepare and spread out all the fish in a shallow dish, flesh side up. Wipe with a damp cloth. Then pour the dressing over them, and leave for 30 minutes. Drain over the dish, reserving the dressing for basting. Place the fish, skin side down, on a well-greased grill, 10–15 cm/4–6 in above medium-hot coals. Cook for 15–20 minutes or until the flesh at the thickest part flakes easily when prodded with a fork.

Shortly before the end of the cooking time, heat the butter and chopped nuts in a small saucepan on the grill.

When the fish are done, lift them off the grill carefully with a wide spatula or slice. Serve each with a spoonful of almond butter poured over it.

FRUIT AND VEGETABLES

FRUIT BASICS

Foil-wrapped Fruit

Foil-wrapped fruit go well with meat, poultry or fish, or can be served as dessert to complete your barbecue dinner. You only need to heat them for a short time on the grill. The recipes below make four average helpings each.

Peaches

INGREDIENTS	Metric	Imperial	American
Medium-sized peaches	*4*	*4*	*4*
Lemon juice	*2 tsp*	*2 tsp*	*2 tsp*
Butter or margarine	*1 tbsp*	*1 tbsp*	*1 tbsp*
Light brown sugar	*2 tbsp*	*2 tbsp*	*2 tbsp*

Peel the peaches and remove stones; slice and lay on heavy-duty foil. Sprinkle with lemon juice, dot with fat, and sprinkle with sugar. Seal tightly in foil, and place on the grill 10–15 cm/4–6 in above hot or medium-hot coals. Cook, moving the packet several times, for 6–8 minutes or until well heated through. Serve with ham or poultry, or for dessert as a topping for ice-cream or sponge cake.

Pineapple

INGREDIENTS	Metric	Imperial	American
Whole fresh pineapple	*1*	*1*	*1*
Clear honey	*3–4 tbsp*	*3–4 tbsp*	*3–4 tbsp*

Peel and core the fruit and cut it into 8 spears lengthways. (Quarter it lengthways to core it, then cut each quarter in half lengthways.) Place the spears on heavy-duty foil. Trickle the honey over them, then seal the packet tightly. Place on the grill, 10–5 cm/4–6 in above hot or medium-hot coals. Cook, moving the package occasionally, for 8–10 minutes or until heated through. Serve with ham or pork, or as a 'starter' at a midday brunch barbecue.

Apples

INGREDIENTS

	Metric	Imperial	American
Medium-sized apples	4	4	4
Lemon juice	2 tsp	2 tsp	2 tsp
Butter or margarine	2 tbsp	2 tbsp	2 tbsp
Sugar	1 tbsp	1 tbsp	1 tbsp
Ground cinnamon or coriander to taste			

Wash the apples, and peel them if you wish, then slice them. Lay them on a large sheet of heavy-duty foil in one layer. Sprinkle them with the lemon juice, dot with fat, then sprinkle with sugar and your chosen spice. Wrap closely in the foil. Place the package on the grill 10–15 cm/4–6 in above hot or medium-hot coals. Cook, moving the package to a new spot occasionally, for 12–15 minutes, or until well heated through and cooked as you prefer. Serve with barbecued pork or as dessert with a dollop of sweetened whipped cream or soured cream.

Bananas

INGREDIENTS

		Metric	Imperial	American
Medium-sized bananas		4	4	4
Butter or margarine)	if using	1 tbsp	1 tbsp	1 tbsp
Sugar)	peeled	1 tsp	1 tsp	1 tsp
Ground cinnamon)	bananas	1 tsp	1 tsp	1 tsp
OR		**OR**	**OR**	**OR**
Clear honey (if using unpeeled bananas)		4 tbsp	4 tbsp	4 tbsp

Peel and quarter or slice the bananas, and place on heavy-duty foil. Dot with butter or margarine and sprinkle with sugar and cinnamon. Alternatively, simply make a slit about 7.5 cm/3 in long in the skin of each banana, trickle 1 tbsp honey into each slit and leave to stand for 30 minutes, cut side up; then place on individual pieces of heavy-duty foil.

Wrap peeled or unpeeled fruit tightly in the foil, and place on the grill 10–15 cm/4–6 in above hot or medium-hot coals. Cook, moving the package(s) several times, for 5–8 minutes if using peeled fruit, or for 8–10 minutes if using unpeeled fruit. Make sure the bananas are well heated through. Serve as a dessert.

Oranges

INGREDIENTS	Metric	Imperial	American
Large seedless oranges	3 or 4	3 or 4	3 or 4
Butter or margarine	1 tbsp	1 tbsp	1 tbsp
Sugar	1 tsp	1 tsp	1 tsp
Ground cinnamon	1 tsp	1 tsp	1 tsp
OR	**OR**	**OR**	**OR**
Dried rosemary leaves	1 tsp	1 tsp	1 tsp

Peel the oranges, divide into segments and place on heavy-duty foil.
Dot with the fat, and sprinkle with the sugar and spice or rosemary
leaves. Seal in the foil, and place on the grill 10–15 cm/4–6 in above
hot or medium-hot coals. Cook, moving the package occasionally,
for 6–8 minutes or until well heated through. Serve with poultry,
beef or fish.

Pears

INGREDIENTS		Metric	Imperial	American
Large dessert pears		4	4	4
Lemon juice	)	2 tsp	2 tsp	2 tsp
Butter or margarine	) If using	1 tbsp	1 tbsp	1 tbsp
Sugar	) sliced	1 tsp	1 tsp	1 tsp
Ground ginger	) pears	1 tsp	1 tsp	1 tsp
OR		**OR**	**OR**	**OR**
Slivered preserved stem	)			
ginger	)	½ tsp	½ tsp	½ tsp
OR		**OR**	**OR**	**OR**
Butter or margarine	) If using	4 tsp	4 tsp	4 tsp
Sugar	) whole	2 tsp	2 tsp	2 tsp
Ground ginger	) pears	2 tsp	2 tsp	2 tsp

Peel and core the pears. Slice them if you wish, and place the slices
on a large sheet of heavy-duty foil. Sprinkle with the lemon juice,
then dot with fat and sprinkle with sugar and with ground or slivered
ginger.

Alternatively, leave the peeled, cored pears whole, and lay on
individual sheets of foil. Fill each core hole with 1 tsp fat, ½ tsp each
sugar and ground ginger.

Wrap the sliced or whole fruit tightly in the foil. Place on the grill
10–15 cm/4–6 in above hot or medium-hot coals. Cook, moving the
package(s) occasionally, for 5–7 minutes if using sliced fruit, or for
10–12 minutes, if using whole fruit. Make sure that whole pears are
well heated through. Serve as a dessert with a dollop of sweetened
whipped cream or ice cream.

VEGETABLE BASICS

Foil-Wrapped Vegetables

Foil-wrapping is the simplest way to prepare vegetables for barbecuing. You can choose from several different seasonings and various garnishes such as chopped parsley or other fresh herbs; or you may decide just to season the vegetables with salt and pepper, or to top them with a little butter. A few garnishing ideas are suggested in the recipes below. Each recipe makes 4 average helpings.

Wash any vegetable well, but do not dry it; the extra moisture is enough to steam-cook most vegetables. Wrap tightly in heavy-duty foil, then place on the grill directly over the coals.

Carrots

INGREDIENTS	Metric	Imperial	American
Medium-sized carrots	450 g	1 lb	1 lb
Salt and pepper			
Butter or margarine	2 tbsp	2 tbsp	2 tbsp
Grated lemon rind	1 tbsp	1 tbsp	1 tbsp

Cut the carrots into 2.5 cm/1 in pieces if you wish. Place on heavy-duty foil. Season with salt and pepper to taste, and dot with the fat. Sprinkle the lemon rind on top. Wrap tightly, and place on the grill 10–15 cm/4–6 in above medium-hot coals. Cook, moving the packet occasionally, for 15–20 minutes for sliced carrots or 25–30 minutes for whole carrots. (Old carrots may need longer.)

Green Peas

INGREDIENTS	Metric	Imperial	American
Green peas in pods	900 g	2 lb	2 lb
Mushrooms, thinly sliced	25 g	1 oz	1 oz
Salt and pepper			
Butter or margarine	2 tbsp	2 tbsp	2 tbsp

Shell the peas, rinse well, and place on heavy-duty foil. Scatter the thinly sliced mushrooms on top, season to taste and dot with fat. Wrap tightly, and place on the grill, 10–15 cm/4–6 in above medium-hot coals. Cook, moving the package occasionally, for about 20 minutes or until tender to bite on.

Courgette-Tomato Casserole (Zucchini-Tomato Casserole)

INGREDIENTS	Metric	Imperial	American
Medium-sized courgettes (zucchini)	2	2	2
Medium-sized tomatoes, skinned	2	2	2
Medium-sized onion, thinly sliced	1	1	1
Salt and pepper			
Oregano leaves	½ tsp	½ tsp	½ tsp
Olive oil or salad oil	1 tbsp	1 tbsp	1 tbsp

Wash the courgettes (zucchini) and cut into 1 cm/½ in rounds. Cut the tomatoes into thin wedges. Arrange half the courgette rounds, tomato wedges and onion jumbled together in an even layer on heavy-duty foil. Season, and sprinkle with ¼ tsp oregano. Repeat the layer on top of the first, using all the remaining vegetables. Season again, and sprinkle with remaining oregano. Pour the oil over the vegetables. Seal tightly in the foil, and place on the grill 10–15 cm/4–6 in above medium-hot coals. Cook, moving the package occasionally, for 25–30 minutes or until done as you wish when pierced with a skewer.

Globe Artichokes

INGREDIENTS	Metric	Imperial	American
Globe artichokes	4	4	4
Olive oil or salad oil	2 tsp	2 tsp	2 tsp
Thinly sliced mild onion	4 tbsp	4 tbsp	4 tbsp
Salt and pepper			
Lemon wedges			

Snip off the top third of each artichoke and the tips of all the remaining leaves. Wash thoroughly, pulling the leaves apart slightly as you wash. Place on individual sheets of heavy-duty foil. Open out the centre leaves slightly and pour ½ tsp oil into the centre of each artichoke. Sprinkle the onion on the tops of the artichokes, and season to taste. Wrap tightly, and place on the grill 10–15 cm/4–6 in above medium-hot coals. Cook, moving the packages occasionally, for 55–60 minutes or until the bottom of each artichoke is tender when pierced with a skewer. Garnish with lemon wedges.

New Potatoes

INGREDIENTS	Metric	Imperial	American
Small new potatoes	450 g	1 lb	1 lb
Salt and pepper			
Finely chopped parsley	2 tsp	2 tsp	2 tsp
Butter or margarine	2 tbsp	2 tbsp	2 tbsp

Wash the potatoes well, and take off a strip of skin (2.5 cm/1 in wide on larger potatoes) all the way round the circumference. Place the potatoes together on heavy-duty foil. Season with salt and pepper, and sprinkle with parsley. Dot with fat. Wrap tightly, and place on the grill 10–15 cm/4–6 in above medium-hot coals. Cook, moving the package occasionally, for 50–55 minutes or until tender when pierced with a skewer.

Green Beans

INGREDIENTS	Metric	Imperial	American
Green beans	450 g	1 lb	1 lb
Salt and pepper			
Fresh or dried savory leaves	1 tsp	1 tsp	1 tsp
Butter or margarine	2 tbsp	2 tbsp	2 tbsp
Toasted flaked almonds	2 tbsp	2 tbsp	2 tbsp

Top and tail the beans, and string if required. Wash and place on heavy-duty foil. Season with salt and pepper, and sprinkle with savory. Dot with fat. Wrap tightly, and place on the grill 10–15 cm/4–6 in above medium-hot coals. Cook, moving the package occasionally, for about 20 minutes or until done as you like them when pierced with a skewer. Just before serving, sprinkle with the almonds.

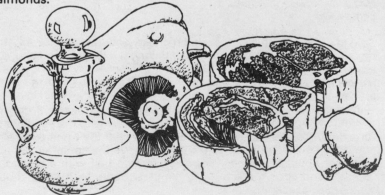

OTHER VEGETABLE RECIPES

Barbecued Baked Beans

INGREDIENTS	Metric	Imperial	American
Streaky bacon rashers (strips) with rind removed	125 g	4 oz	4 oz
Butter or margarine	25 g	1 oz	1 oz
Celery sticks, finely chopped	2	2	2
Medium-sized onion, chopped	1	1	1
Can of baked beans	447-g can	15¾-oz can	15¾-oz can
Horseradish sauce	1 tbsp	1 tbsp	1 tbsp
French mustard	1 tsp	1 tsp	1 tsp

Cut the bacon into small pieces and place in a heavy flameproof pan on the barbecue grill, 10–15 cm/4–6 in above the cooler coals. Heat until the fat starts to run. Add the fat, and the finely chopped celery and onion. Cook gently until golden, stirring occasionally.

Add the beans, horseradish sauce and mustard. Cover and heat through over medium-hot coals until the beans are piping hot. Serve with sausages or hamburgers.

Cheesy-Topped Tomatoes

INGREDIENTS	Metric	Imperial	American
Medium-sized tomatoes	8	8	8
Salad oil			
Medium-sized onion	1	1	1
Finely chopped parsley	4 tbsp	4 tbsp	4 tbsp
Soft white breadcrumbs	75 g	3 oz	1½ cups
Salt and black pepper			
Small thin squares of cheese	16	16	16

Cut the tomatoes in half across, and scoop out the seeds. Brush the insides with oil. Chop the onion finely, and mix with the parsley and breadcrumbs. Season to taste, and use to stuff the tomato halves.

Place on the grill 10–15 cm/4–6 in above the cooler coals, and cook for about 5 minutes. Top each tomato half with a square of cheese, and cook for another 5 minutes. Serve with lamb chops, burgers or sausages.

Double-Covered Onions

INGREDIENTS	Metric	Imperial	American
Large onions, 340–400 g/12–14 oz each			

For each onion
Butter for greasing
Salt

	Metric	Imperial	American
Grated cheese or soured cream or Two-Way Yoghurt Dressing (page 41)	*1 tbsp*	*1 tbsp*	*1 tbsp*

Cut out squares of foil which will each enclose an onion completely. Grease them well. Cut off the roots of the onions but do not skin them. Cut a deep cross in the top of each onion, almost down to the centre. Place one onion in the middle of each foil square and draw the foil up, twisting the edges into a knot over the top of the onion. Bake the onions in the oven at 180°C/350°F/Gas Mark 4 for about 1 hour until nearly cooked. Transfer to the barbecue and complete the cooking in the hot coals at the edge of the fire. Place each onion on a plate, open the foil, and fold back the brown skin. Open out the cut onion flesh a little with a spoon, then cover with the chosen topping and eat with a fork.

Yellow Rice

INGREDIENTS	Metric	Imperial	American
Water	*650 ml*	*1¼ pt*	*3 cups*
Long-grain rice	*200 g*	*7 oz*	*1 cup*
Cinnamon stick	*1*	*1*	*1*
Turmeric	*½ tsp*	*½ tsp*	*½ tsp*
Salt	*1 tsp*	*1 tsp*	*1 tsp*
Butter or margarine	*2 tbsp*	*2 tbsp*	*2 tbsp*
Seedless raisins (optional)	*75 g*	*3 oz*	*½ cup*
Ground cinnamon			
Pepper			

Ahead of time, bring the water to the boil in a large saucepan. Sprinkle in the rice. Reduce the heat to low, and add the cinnamon stick, turmeric, a little salt, 1 tbsp of the fat and the raisins if used. Stir round, then cook until the water is absorbed and the rice is tender. Add a little more water if needed to prevent it drying out. Transfer the pan to the barbecue to keep warm; remove the cinnamon stick, and stir round with a fork to separate any grains which stick together, then cover. Shortly before serving, add the remaining butter, a little ground cinnamon and salt and pepper to taste. Let the fat melt before serving.

Ratatouille

INGREDIENTS	Metric	Imperial	American
Butter or margarine	25 g	1 oz	2 tbsp
Olive oil	3 tbsp	3 tbsp	3 tbsp
Large onions, thinly sliced	2	2	2
Garlic cloves, crushed	2	2	2
Medium-sized aubergines (eggplant) thinly sliced	3	3	3
Large green pepper, seeded and chopped	1	1	1
Large sweet red pepper, seeded and chopped	1	1	1
Medium-sized courgettes (zucchini) sliced	5	5	5
Can of tomatoes	396-g can	14-oz can	14-oz can
Dried basil leaves	1 tsp	1 tsp	1 tsp
Dried rosemary leaves	1 tsp	1 tsp	1 tsp
Bay leaves	2	2	2
Salt	1½ tsp	1½ tsp	1½ tsp
Black pepper	¾ tsp	¾ tsp	¾ tsp
Chopped parsley	2 tbsp	2 tbsp	2 tbsp

In a large flameproof casserole, melt the fat with the oil over moderate heat. Add the onions and garlic, and fry, stirring occasionally, for about 5 minutes or until the onions are soft. Add the aubergine (eggplant) slices, green and red peppers, and courgette (zucchini) slices to the casserole. Fry for 4–5 minutes, shaking the casserole frequently. Add the tomatoes and juice from the can, the basil, rosemary, bay leaves and seasoning. Sprinkle with the parsley. Bring to the boil. Cover.

Transfer to the grill 10–15 cm/4–6 in over medium-hot coals, and simmer for 40–50 minutes until the vegetables are cooked. Serve from the casserole at once, as a vegetable dish, as a basting sauce for meat or poultry, or as a first course. Serves 4–6.

Chip-'N-Chutney Cheesy Potatoes

INGREDIENTS	Metric	Imperial	American
Filling			
Thick coating white sauce	300 ml	$\frac{1}{2}$ pt	1$\frac{1}{4}$ cups
Grated cheese	175 g	6 oz	$\frac{3}{4}$ cup firmly packed
Salt and pepper			
Mild chutney (sweet pickle)	4 tbsp	4 tbsp	4 tbsp
Chipolata sausages, (small fresh pork sausages or franks) cooked and chopped	450 g	1 lb	1 lb
Spuds			
Equal-sized large baking potatoes	12	12	12
Oil for brushing			

Heat the filling ingredients gently in a saucepan, then turn into a vacuum flask and seal. Brush the potatoes with oil, wrap in foil. Bake them for 2 hours in the glowing ash at the edge of a camp-fire or among the coals at the edge of a big barbecue. Alternatively, bake them in the oven before barbecuing and transfer to the barbecue when the fire is established to complete the cooking. Open the foil just enough to let you slit the potatoes open; pile chip-'n-chutney cheese mixture into each. Serve with spoons.

A super backstop dish to have ready to cope with extra-hearty appetites or numbers — or in case the rain comes down.

Bacon-Wrapped Corn

INGREDIENTS	Metric	Imperial	American
Corn on the cob	8	8	8
Middle cut bacon rashers (strips) without rind	8	8	8
Salt and pepper			
Butter	8 tbsp	8 tbsp	8 tbsp

Remove the husks and silk of the corn if needed. Wrap each cob in a bacon rasher (strip), and place if on a square of diamond foil. Sprinkle it with seasoning and top it with 15 ml/1 tbsp butter. Fold the foil round it to make a parcel. Cook on the barbecue for 45 minutes, turning often. Unfold the foil for serving.

INDEX